To Know the Love of Christ

"And to know the love of Christ, which passeth knowledge, that ye might be filled with all the fulness of God." **Ephesians 3:19**

Justin Hopkins

Library of Congress Control Number: 2011963540
Version 1.0

Discover Other Titles
By Hopkins Publishing
HopkinsPublishing.com

Free Downloads

All of the lessons contained in this book are available as a free download. This title is also available as a free eBook for most e-reading devices.

justinandleahhopkins.com/Study

What Others Are Saying...

The "Love of Christ" Bible studies are revolutionary to our day and age. The study stops the mouths of teachers and allows the students to get into to Scriptures. It is this century's "Thus Saith the Lord" Bible Study. There are simply no opinions, feelings or personal beliefs, but it forces the student to the Scriptures and the Scriptures only. I highly recommend these studies to anyone who is searching or wishing to teach Jesus Christ and Him only.

– Steven Patterson, Minister, Gonzales, TX

"To Know the Love of Christ" is my most valuable tool in evangelizing. It is so simple that anyone in the congregation can use them and my success rate has been around 98%.... It forces the student to be honest with themselves and admit that the Bible is our only guide. Not only that, these lessons deal with a problem that we've faced in the Lord's church for years and that is what the new convert is to do after baptism in order to grow and be rooted and grounded in the Truth.

– Jim Word, Minister, Natalia, TX

It is very practical and simple while being deep and thorough. It gives the evangelist the opportunity to gain rapport with a prospect while holding them accountable to investigate their professed faith with the Bible.

– Shawn Price, Minister, Leakey, TX

The lessons came straight out of the Bible and were very thorough. I was given an answer for all of my questions straight from the Scriptures.

– Walter Starr

Acknowledgments

There are many who have contributed to the creation of these studies in various ways. To all of them I owe a great debt of gratitude. There were several who contributed in various ways, some large, some small, who desire to remain nameless. You know who you are, and so does our Heavenly Father. Thank you.

Rudy Cain at World Video Bible School (wvbs.org) has graciously given permission for the use of images developed for the Searching For Truth series. On that note, Searching For Truth provides another excellent resource. I would encourage all to check it out at searchingfortruth.org.

Rick Brumback, director of Southwest School of Bible Studies (swsbs.edu) also was gracious in allowing me to use images that he created for a PowerPoint sermon.

My wonderful bride, Leah Hopkins, spent countless hours proof reading these lessons and giving me suggestions for their improvement. Thank you, honey. I love you.

Contents

Introduction

These lessons are designed to be used for independent study, study with a partner, or in a small class setting. When studying through these lessons, be sure and get everybody in the room involved. Always approach your study with prayer, and on open heart and mind, that you may find God's Truth as it is revealed.

As you study, take turns reading the passages of Scripture, and then reading the questions that follow. Then, from the passage, find the answer. If you are having trouble with a question, re-read the passage. The answer is there! Then write your answer in the blank provided.

These lessons were developed using the King James Version of the Bible. They work most fluidly when that translation is used, but any English translation should be acceptable.

As you go through these studies, if you see something that you feel might be improved or changed in some way, please drop me an email and let me know. **Justin@hopkinspublishing.com** Thanks!

Lesson 1

Knowing Christ and His Authority in Religion

How do we obtain the Whole Truth?

When we look at Scripture, we must take into account all that Scripture says about a matter. While two Scriptures will not contradict one another, they may *complement* one another, each adding more information to the other. This exercise illustrates that principle.

Scripture	Mark 14:47	Matthew 26:51	Luke 22:50-51	John 18:10
Who?				
Drew What?				
Did What?				
To Whom?				
The Whole Story				

1. John 8:32 What will make you free? _____

2. John 4:24 Must you worship God with all of your heart (in spirit)? _____

    a. Must you worship God in truth? _____

3. John 17:17 What is truth? _____

    a. Does that mean that we must worship and serve God based upon what His Word says? _____

Your Salvation Experience

1. Do you feel that you are saved at this moment? _____

2. Please tell me about your salvation experience:

3. Did you make a commitment to be a Christian? _____

    a. When? _____

4. Did you make a confession? _____

    a. If so, what did you confess? _____

5. Were you baptized? _____

    a. How long after your commitment? _____

    b. How? _____

    c. Why? _____

6. At what moment in time did you become saved? _____

_____

7. What did you do that "caused" you to become saved? _____

_____

8. Were you saved before or after you were baptized? _____

_____

Finding Common Ground
Answer: Yes, No, Unsure

1. Do you believe in the God of the Bible? _____

2. Do you believe the Bible came from God? _____

3. Do you believe the **entire** Bible is true? _____

4. Do you believe Jesus Christ is the Son of God? _____

5. Do you believe Jesus Christ died and rose from the dead?

_____

6. Do you believe Jesus Christ has **all** authority in Heaven and on Earth? _____

7. Did Jesus ever make a promise which He did not fulfill?

_____

8. Do you believe in a Heaven where people will be rewarded eternally? _____

9. Do you believe in a Hell where people will be punished eternally? _____

10. Do you believe that **all people** will stand in judgment before God? _____

11. If we followed **just the Bible**, nothing more, nothing less, do you believe we could make it to Heaven? _____

12. Do you believe all Churches **should** teach the same thing?

_____

13. Do you believe all Churches **do** teach the same thing? _____

14. Do all Churches belong to God? _____

15. If not, how many Churches do belong to God? _____

16. Do you believe that Jesus is the **only** source of salvation?

_____

The importance of knowing Jesus and His love

1. John 17:2-3 Must we know Jesus to have eternal life? _____

2. 2 Thessalonians 1:8 Are there consequences for not knowing God and not obeying the Gospel of Christ? _____

Does Jesus have any authority in our life today?

1. John 14:23·24 From where did Jesus get His teachings? _____

_____

2. Hebrews 1:1-2 Today God speaks to us through _____

3. John 3:35 Over how many things has God given Jesus authority? _____

4. Matthew 28:18 How much authority does Jesus have? _____

    a. Is there anything over which Jesus does **not** have authority?

_____

b. Is there any authority left anywhere for anybody else?

_____

5. John 17:2 Jesus has authority over _____.

6. Ephesians 1:20-23 Jesus is head over all things to the _____

_____.

How much authority does Jesus have over the church? _____

7. John 12:48 Whose words will we be judged by? _____

a. Will we be judged by our own feelings, opinions, or

beliefs?_____

b. Will we be judged by our family or friends? _____

c. Will we be judged by preachers or the Church? _____

d. Will we be judged by manmade creeds or books? _____

8. John 6:68 Who has the words of eternal life? _____

a. Should we go to anyone else (parents, preachers, relatives,

friend) for eternal life? _____

9. Acts 3:22-23 What will happen to those who do not listen to the all-authoritative words of Jesus? _____

Did the Holy Spirit guide the Apostles into All Truth?

1. John 14:26 Did Jesus say the Holy Spirit would teach them all things and bring all that Jesus said to their remembrance?

_____

a. When the Apostles taught by inspiration of the Holy Spirit, were they teaching their own words or the words of Jesus?

_____

2. John 16:13-14 How much truth did the Holy Spirit reveal to the apostles? _____

a. Where did the Holy Spirit get His truth? _____

b. Is there anything that we would need to know that the Holy Spirit did **not** reveal to the apostles? _____

Where is Christ's all-authoritative Word today?

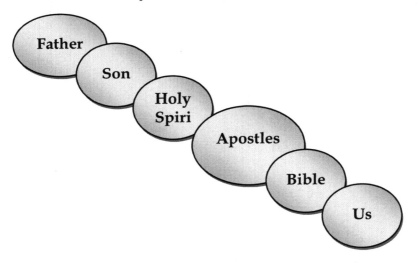

1. 1 John 1:1-4 Were the apostles credible first-hand witnesses of Jesus' all-authoritative words (the Word of life)? _____

a. Did the apostles write down that all-authoritative Word?

_____

b. Does receiving that Word give us fellowship with the apostles? _____

c. Does receiving that Word give us fellowship with God and Christ? _____

2. 2 Timothy 3:16-17 Does the Bible thoroughly furnish us unto every good work? _____

a. Do we need additional revelations to make us complete before God? _____

b. Do we need the Book of Mormon to make us complete spiritually? _____

c. Do we need Church Traditions, Manuals, Creed Books, Confessions of Faith to make us complete spiritually?

_____

3. 2 Peter 1:3 Has God given us all things that pertain to life and godliness? _____

a. Since God has given us all things that pertain to life and godliness in the Bible, should any other source be used as our religious authority? _____

b. Is there anything that we need to know which has not been included in Christ's all-authoritative, all-sufficient, written Word? _____

Should we add to or take away from God's Word?

1. 1 Peter 4:11 Should we teach or authorize anything I religion that is not taught or authorized in God's Word? _____

2. 1 Corinthians 1:10 Should the way we think in religion be guided only by God's Word? _____

a. Should how we speak in religion be guided only by God's Word? _____

b. Should how we act (our judgment) in religion be guided only by God's Word? _____

3. Leviticus 10:1-2 Did Nadab and Abihu offer fire which God had not commanded them to offer, even though He had *not prohibited* its use? _____

a. Did they alter God's commandments? _____

b. Was God pleased with them? _____

c. Must we be careful how we handle the word of God? _____

_____

4. 2 John 9-11 If we do not abide in the doctrine of Christ, is God pleased? _____

a. Do you want to please God? _____

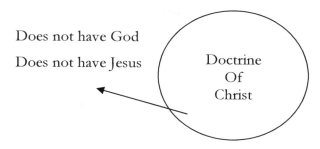

Does not have God

Does not have Jesus

5. Galatians1:6-9 Is God pleased if we **add** anything to His Word?

_____

   a. Is God pleased if we **subtract** anything from His Word?

   _____

   b. Is God pleased if we **change** anything in His Word?

   _____

   c. What would happen to an **angel** if he tampered with God's

   Word? _____

   d. What would happen to an **apostle** if he tampered with

   God's Word? _____

   e. What would happen to **us** if we tampered with God's Word?

   _____

6. Matthew 15:9 Their worship to God was unacceptable because

   they taught for doctrines _____

   a. Will our worship be acceptable if we alter Christ's all-

   authoritative Word? _____

7. Matthew 7:21-23 Did these people think that they were doing

   good works? _____

a. What kind of work did Christ say they were actually doing?

_____

b. What must we do if we want to enter Heaven? _____

_____

c. Do you want to enter Heaven? _____

Are we under the Old Testament Law today?

1. Hebrews 1: 1·2 Through who did God speak to the fathers in the past? _____

   a. Who is the only authorized spokesman for God today?

_____

2. John 12:48 Whose words will be used to judge us in the last day?

_____

3. Hebrews 9:15-17 Is Jesus the mediator of the New Testament?

_____

   a. When did the New Testament of Jesus go into effect?

_____

4. Hebrews 5:8-9 Was it before or after Jesus suffered and died that His Law and saving power came into effect?

_____

   a. Who does Jesus offer salvation? _____

5. Hebrews 8:6-7 Is Jesus the mediator of a better covenant?

_____

   a. If the Old Testament completely fulfilled God's Will would He have created the New Testament? _____

6. Hebrews 8: 13 When God gave the NEW covenant, did he make the first one OLD (no longer in force)? _____

7. Colossians 2:14 When was the bond written in ordinances (Old Testament) abolished? _____

8. Galatians 5:4 Can we be saved by Christ if we try to justify teachings or practices by the Old Testament? _____

   a. Is the New Testament the law which is spiritually binding today? _____

Summary

1. We must hear all of what Scripture has to say about any subject.

    a. Two Scriptures will not contradict one another

    b. Two Scriptures may complement one another and add more information.

2. We must know Jesus and obey Him if we wish to be saved.

3. Jesus received all authority from God:

    1) In heaven and on earth,

    2) Over all flesh,

    3) Over the church.

3. We will be judged by the teachings of Jesus.

4. The Apostles were inspired by the Holy Spirit in what they taught and wrote.

5. The Inspired word is our only all-authoritative, all-sufficient guide in religion.

6. We must not add to or take away from Gods word.

7. The New Testament is the law which we are under and by which we will be judged.

Lesson 2
The Church that Jesus Built

The Church

1. Matthew 16:18 Who built the Church? _____

   a. To whom does the Church belong? _____

   b. How many Churches did Jesus build? _____

2. Ephesians 1:20-23 Is Jesus the head over all things to the

   Church? _____

   a. In verse 23 the Church is also called his _____

3. Ephesians 4:4 How many "hopes" do we have? _____

   a. How many Holy Spirits are there? _____

   b. How many Bodies (Churches) are there? _____

5. 1 Corinthians 1:10 Is religious division condemned? _____
   a. Since religious division is condemned and since Jesus prayed
   that all his followers be one, must we strive to be one
   religiously? _____

The Body of Christ – Modern View

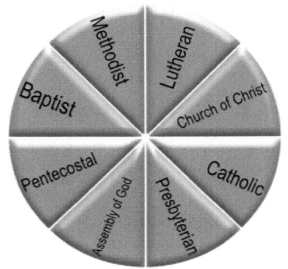

The Body of Christ – God's View

John 17:20-22

1 Corinthians 1:10

One Origin
One Teaching
One Practice

Used by Permission: Rick Brumback

6. Colossians 1:18

Since Jesus is the head of the church, the body, should we go to anyone other than Jesus and the inspired writers of the New Testament to learn the organization, worship and name of his church? _____

The Organization of the Church

1. Matthew 15:13

Must we follow the pattern that Jesus laid out in His

commandments in order to please God? _____

2. Acts 14:23 Did these inspired apostles appoint Elders in every

church? _____

a. Would we be pleasing to God if we do as they did by

ordaining a plurality of Elders in every congregation?

_____

b. Could we be wrong if we did NOT follow their Biblical

example in organizing the Church? _____

3. Acts 20:17, 28 Are the Elders to be the overseers of the church?

_____

4. Titus 1:5-7 When Paul told Titus to set in order what was

lacking, did he tell him to ordain Elders? _____

a. When we do what Titus did in organizing the church, are we

doing the will of God? _____

b. Do the terms "Elder", "Bishop" and "Overseer" refer to the

same office? _____

5. 1 Timothy 3:1-7 Must an Elder meet certain qualifications?

_____

    a. Must an Elder be married? _____

    b. Must an Elder have children? _____

    c. May a recent convert (novice) serve as an Elder? _____

6. 1 Timothy 3:8-12 What church official is now being discussed

(v. 8)? _____

    b. Is it God's plan that there be qualified Elders and Deacons

in every church? _____

7. Philippians 1:1 The church at Philippi was organized with

_____ and _____.

Christ
(Head)

Elders
(Overseers, Bishops)
Deacons
Saints
(Christians)

8. **Hebrews 13:17** Are Christians commanded to submit to the authority of the Elders (as long as they do not add to, take away from, or make substitutions to God's Word)? _____

9. **1 Peter 5:3** Are the Elders (Bishops) to lead the Church by example or by absolute control? _____

The Worship of the Church

Types of Worship

1. **John 4:24** Must we worship the correct God (and know who He is)? _____

   a. Must we worship God in spirit (with the correct attitude)?

   _____

   b. Must we worship God in truth? _____

2. **John 17:17** What is truth? _____

   a. Since we must worship God in truth, must we worship as God has directed in the Bible? _____

3. **Matthew 15:9** Is it possible to worship God in vain? _____

   a. If we worship God according to the commandments of uninspired men, will God accept it? _____

4. **Acts 17:22-23** Is it possible to worship God ignorantly? _____

   _____

   a. If we do so, will our worship be acceptable to God? _____

   _____

Acts of Worship

1. **Acts 2:42** The disciples continued steadfastly in

   _____, _____ and the

   _____

   _____

   a. Will we be pleasing to God if we regularly do these things?

   _____

2. **Luke 22:19-20** Did Jesus command his disciples to partake of

   the Lord's Supper? _____

   a. What is the purpose of partaking of the Lord's Supper?

   _____

3. **1 Corinthians 10:16**

   a. The cup is a communion of the _____ of Christ.

   b. The bread is a communion of the _____ of Christ.

4. **Acts 20:7** When God told the Israelites in Exodus 20:8 to

   remember the Sabbath, did he mean for them to keep every

   Sabbath? _____

   a. When those Christians met upon the first day of the week to

   eat the Lord's Supper, did they do it on the first day of each

   week? _____

   b. Should Christians today eat the Lord's Supper upon the first

   day of the week? _____

9. **1 Corinthians 16:1-2** Is it God's will that we give based on how

much we have earned each week?_____

a. Are we to make a contribution on the same day we are to partake of the Lord's Supper? _____

10. **Ephesians 5:19** Are we to sing? _____

a. This passage specifies the instrument that we are to use to make melody. We are to make melody in _____

_____

b. Does this passage mention mechanical instruments of music? _____

c. Church historians tell us that the followers of Christ did not use mechanical instruments of music in their worship for hundreds of years after Christ.

d. When you attend the worship of the church of Christ, you will notice we do not use instrumental music in our worship.

The following comparisons help to illustrate the reason:

11. **Genesis 6:14** – God told Noah, "Make thee an ark of

_____."

a. Would Noah have sinned if he had built the ark of any other wood? _____

b. Would Noah have sinned if he had used Gopher wood AND Maple or Pine to build the ark? _____

c. When God said, "Gopher wood," that automatically eliminated any other kind of wood.

d. When God said, "Sing," that automatically eliminated any other kind of music.

11. Leviticus 10:1-2 God had specified what fire to use (Leviticus 16:12), but He had NOT told them "don't use any other fire."

    a. Did Nadab and Abihu sin when they offered a different kind of fire other than God commanded? _____

    b. Did God punish them?_____

    c. Is it important to worship God the way HE has commanded without alteration? _____

12. Matthew 26:26-29 Would it be a sin to use pie instead of bread for the Lord's Supper? _____

    a. Would it be a sin to serve soda on the Lord's Supper instead of the fruit of the vine? _____

    b. Would it be a sin to add hamburgers and milkshakes to the Lord's Supper? _____

    c. If we were to change our worship in any of these ways would it make our worship vain (useless)? _____

    d. If we were to change our worship in any of these ways would we be abiding in the Doctrine of Christ? _____

The Name of the Church

1. Matthew 16:18 Who built the church? _____

    a. To whom did Jesus say the Church would belong? _____

_____

2. Acts 20:28 Who purchased the church with His blood?

_____

a. Whose name should be on the "deed"? _____

3. 1 Corinthians 1:10-13 Is it a sin to name the church after Paul, Apollos, Cephas, or any other human being? _____

    a. If the church were named after Paul, whom would we be glorifying? _____

    b. To name the Church after a man would mean that:

Christ is _____

That man was _____ for us.

We would be _____ in the name of that man.

    c. If the church were named after a religious act such as "Repentance", what would it be glorifying? _____

    d. If it were a sin to name it the "Pauline Church", would it be a sin to name it the "Lutheran Church"? _____

    f. If it were a sin to name it the "Repentance Church", would it be a sin to name it the "Baptist Church"?

_____

    g. Can you think of other unauthorized religious names that are used today? _____

_____

4. Colossians 3:17 Are we to do "all" in the name (by the authority) of the Lord Jesus? _____

    b. Would this include the name by which we refer to God's people? _____

5. Romans 16:16 Do you read of the church of Christ in the Bible?

_____

a. Would it be wrong to call the church by this name? _____

b. Would this name glorify the one who built the church and

bought it with his blood? _____

6. **Hebrews 8:5** Was Moses warned to build the tabernacle after

God's pattern? _____

a. Must we be careful to build the church after God's pattern?

_____

Summary

In this lesson we have learned:

1. Jesus is the builder, owner and head of the church.
2. Jesus built only one church.
3. Unity among the followers of Jesus is commanded and division is condemned.
4. We must go to the New Testament to learn the organization, worship and name of the church.
5. God has decreed that there be qualified Elders and Deacons in every congregation.
6. In the worship we are commanded to
   1) Partake of the Lord's Supper on the first day of the week.
   2) Teach God's Word.
   3) Pray.
   4) Sing.
   5) Make a Contribution
7. The name "church of Christ" is Scriptural and would glorify the one who built the church and bought it with his blood.

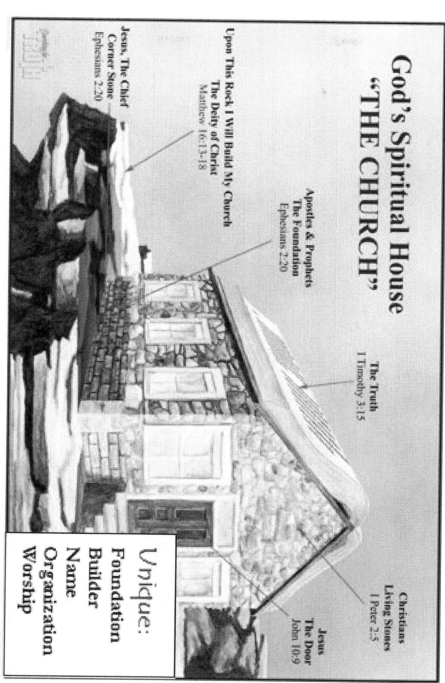

God's Spiritual House
"THE CHURCH"

Apostles & Prophets
The Foundation
Ephesians 2:20

Upon This Rock I Will Build My Church
The Deity of Christ
Matthew 16:13-18

Jesus, The Chief
Corner Stone
Ephesians 2:20

The Truth
1 Timothy 3:15

Christians
Living Stones
1 Peter 2:5

Jesus
The Door
John 10:9

Unique:
Foundation
Builder
Name
Organization
Worship

Lesson 3
Drawing Near to God

Man's Universal Problem, Does it affect me?

1. **Isaiah 59:1-2** What is the only thing that can separate us from God? _____

What is Sin?

1. 1 John 3:4 Sin is _____

2. 1 John 5:17 All _____ is sin.

   a. Romans 1:16-17 Is Righteousness revealed in the Gospel?

   _____

   b. Is it sin to do something that is condemned in the New

   Testament? _____

3. James 4:17 Is it sin to fail to do something that you should?

_____

   a. Have you ever failed to do what you knew was right? _____

4. Romans 14:23

   a. Is it sin to do something that violates your conscience? _____

   b. Have you ever done something that bothered your conscience?

_____

How does sin happen?

1. James 1:14-15 What draws you away and causes you to be

tempted? _____

   a. What happens when you act on that lust? _____

_____

Who is affected by sin?

1. Romans 3:10 How many are righteous? _____

2. Romans 3:23 How many have sinned? _____

   a. Does this include you? _____

What are the Consequences of Sin?

11. Romans 6:23 What are the wages of sin? _____

   a. How many sins must you commit to be lost eternally?

_____

2. 1 Corinthians 6:9-10 Will the unrighteous inherit the kingdom
of God? _____

3. Matthew 5:21-22 Is it a sin to be angry without a cause?

_____

4. Matthew 5:27-28 Is it a sin to look at a man or woman to lust
after them? _____

5. Matthew 5:31-32 Is it a sin to divorce your spouse for a cause
other than adultery? _____

   a. Is it a sin to marry someone who was divorced for the wrong
   reason? _____

6. Matthew 5:33-34 Is it a sin to make a promise and not keep it?

_____

7. Revelation 21:8 What will happen to sinners at the end of the
world? _____

What about God's Justice?

1. Revelation 15:3 Is God just (righteous)? _____

    a. If a Judge refused to sentence convicted criminals, would he be just (righteous)? _____

    b. Does righteousness demand that a Judge sentence convicted criminals? _____

2. Romans 2:11 Is there respect of persons with God? _____

3. 2 Corinthians 5:10 Will every person be judged based upon what they have done? _____

4. Revelation 20:12-15 Were the dead judged according to their works? _____

    a. What happened to those who were not written in the Lamb's book of life? _____

5. 2 Peter 3:9 Is it God's will that you will be lost eternally?

_____

6. Romans 5:8 Did Jesus die for sinners? _____

    a. Was the death of Jesus on the cross an act of God's love for us? _____

7. Romans 5:9 Can we be justified by the blood of Jesus? _____

8. Hebrews 5:9 Is Jesus the author of eternal salvation to those who obey him? _____

    a. Will you be saved if you do not obey Jesus? _____

9. Matthew 7:21-23 Will Jesus save all those who call upon his name? _____

    b. Were these believers lost? _____

    c. According to verse 21, what must one do to go to heaven?

_____

What Must I Do To Be Saved?

God has given us clear ultimatums concerning our salvation. Find the ultimatum in each passage. Example: You must eat OR you will die.

1. Acts 3:22-23 According to these verses you must

_____ or be _____

2. John 8:24 According to this verse you must _____ or

_____ ____ _____ _____

3. Luke 13:3 According to this verse you must

_____ or _____

4. 2 Corinthians 7:9-10 Is merely being sorry for your sins the

repentance God demands? _____

    a. Does repentance demand that you turn from his sins?

_____

5. Matthew 10:32-33 According to this verse you must

_____ or be _____

6. 1 Peter 3:21 The condition of salvation stated here is

_____

7. John 3:5 According to this verse you must be baptized or you

_____ _____ _____ the Kingdom of God.

8. Mark 16:16 Jesus said we must _____ and be

_____ to be saved.

9. Acts 2:38 The inspired preacher told these believers to

_____ and be _____

   a. Repentance and baptism are for _____

10. Ephesians 1:3 Are ALL spiritual blessings in Christ?

_____

   a. If ALL spiritual blessings are IN Christ, are there any spiritual

   blessings outside of Christ? _____

11. 2 Timothy 2:10 Is salvation in Christ? _____

   a. Is it your understanding that one must be IN Christ to be

   saved? _____

12. *Galatians 3:27 How does one get into Christ?* _____

Used by Permission: Rick Brumback

13. Ephesians 4:5 Is there more than one valid baptism in God's

   will? _____

a. Since God accepts only ONE baptism, must we be careful to be sure we are baptized the way GOD says?

_____

14. Acts 8:36-38 Did Philip baptize the Eunuch in water?

_____

a. Did both Philip and the Eunuch go down into the water?

_____

b. Would it have been necessary for both Philip and the Eunuch to go down into the water if sprinkling or pouring were the one baptism God commands?

_____

c.. Would it have been necessary for both Philip and the Eunuch to go down into the water if immersion were the one baptism God commanded? _____

15. 1 Peter 3:21. In the one baptism, must there be the answering of a good conscience toward God?

_____

a. Can a baby conscientiously accept baptism as the command of God? _____

16. Revelation 1:5 How does Jesus wash us from our sins?

_____

17. Acts 22:16 How do we call on the name of the Lord? _____

_____

a. When are our sins washed away? _____

18. Romans 6:3-5 Does the Bible describe the one baptism as a burial in water? _____

   a. Where do we get the benefits of the death of Jesus? _____

_____

   b. *If you are baptized the way the Bible says, could you be wrong?*

_____

   c. If you are NOT baptized the way the Bible says, *could* you be wrong? _____

   d. Do you want to take a chance on missing heaven? _____

   e. Do you believe Jesus Christ is the Son of God? _____

   f. As we have seen, without repentance we will perish. Are you willing to begin making changes in your life as you live for God? _____

   g. Have you been baptized in the name of Jesus Christ:

      For salvation (Acts 2:21)

      For remission of sins (Acts 2:38)

      To be added to the New Testament Church (Acts 2:47)

      (look back at your salvation experience)? _____

19. John 14:15 If we really love Jesus, will we want to obey him?

_____

   a. Do you love him? _____

   b. Do you want to obey him? _____

♦**c.** Since Jesus wants you to be baptized, and now that you understand the importance of being baptized right now, wouldn't it please Jesus for you to be baptized right now?

_____

20. **Ephesians 5:26** How does Jesus sanctify His Church? _____

Used by permission: WVBS

21. 1 Corinthians 6:11 Did these people become sanctified and justified when they were washed (baptized)? _____

22. Titus 3:5 What does Jesus save us by? _____

_____

   a. How does one become sanctified? _____

   b. How does one become justified? _____

   c. How does one become a part of the Church? _____

   d. How does one become saved? _____

   e. Do you want Jesus to save you and add you to His Church?

_____

   ♦**f.** When? _____

23. James 4:13-14 Are you guaranteed to live another day? _____

   a. If you were to die right now are you sure you would go to heaven? _____

   b. Do you want to go to Heaven? _____

24. 2 Corinthians 6:2 When is the accepted time? _____

   a. When is the day of salvation? _____

   b. Has God promised you another day in which to secure your soul? _____

   c. When should you be baptized into Christ? _____

   ♦**d.** Are you ready to be baptized right now? _____

25. 2 Thessalonians 1:7-9 Will Jesus take vengeance on those that do not obey the Gospel? _____

26. Revelation 14:11 Will those people be tormented forever?

_____

a. Will they ever have any rest? _____

b. Do you want to suffer with them for eternity? _____

27. **Revelation 20:12-15** What happens to those who aren't found in the book of life? _____

    a. Is **Your** name written in the Lamb's book of Life? _____

    b. Do you want Jesus to write your name in His book of life?

    _____

    ✦**c.** When? _____

28. **Hebrews 5:8-9** Jesus become the author of eternal salvation to all them that _____

    a. If you understand this you should obey it.

    b. If you do not understand this, then you should not obey it.

    c. Do you understand? _____.

    ✦**d.** Are you ready to obey Jesus' command to be baptized?

What does Obedience require of me?

1. **Luke 14:25-30** Is there *any* human relationship that should stand between you and Christ? _____

    a. Is there *any* human relationship that should be more important to you than serving Christ? _____

    b. Can you be Jesus' follower if you do not follow Him every day of your life? _____

2. **Matthew 6:33** Must we put Christ first in our lives above everything and everybody else? _____

a. Will you promise to put Christ first in your life? _____

3. Hebrews 5:9 Must we obey Jesus to be saved eternally? _____

a. Will you obey Him? _____

4. Revelation 2:10 Must we follow Jesus faithfully in order to be saved? _____

a. How long must we follow Him? _____

5. Hebrews 10:25 Must Christians be faithful in attendance? _____

_____

a. Can a *faithful* Christian miss worship services or Bible class if he or she is physically able to be present? _____

b. Will you be faithful in attending every service of the Lord's Church? _____

c. After you are baptized into Christ, where do you plan to worship? _____

Summary

1. Sin separates man from God.
   a. Sin is: breaking the Law of Christ, committing evil, failing to do good.
   b. Sin happens when we act upon our own wrongful lusts or desires.
   c. Everybody of a sound mind and judgment has been affected by sin.
2. The consequences of sin are death and eternal separation from God.
3. God is just and righteous in His judgments and therefore must punish all sin.
4. God does not want anybody to be lost, and through His mercy has provided a means of salvation.
5. In order to gain salvation we must obey the Gospel plan of salvation and submit our lives to Christ.
6. After becoming a Christian we must live faithfully in order to remain in a saved condition.

Lesson 4
In the Love of Christ

Before I Obeyed the Gospel . . .

I was lost in sin

1. **Isaiah 59:2** What separates us from God? _____.

   a. What hides God's face from us? _____.

2. **Romans 3:23** How many people have sinned? _____.

   a. Does this include you and me? _____.

3. **Ezekiel 18:20** What will happen to the soul that sins? _____.

   _____

I was without hope
1. **Revelation 20:15** What happens to those who are not found in
   the book of life? _____

2. **Ephesians 2:12** Before becoming a Christian:

   a. Did you have Christ? _____

    b. Were you a part of God's people (spiritual Israel)?_____.

    c. Were you a part of the covenant of promise? _____

    d. Did you have hope? _____

    e. Did you have God? _____

3. **Romans 6:23** "For the wages of _____ is _____."

How many sins must a person commit to be lost eternally?

_____

God Showed His Love for Me

1. **Genesis 18:25** Shall not the _____ of all the earth do

_____?

    a. Is God just in His judgments? _____

    b. Would a judge be just if he failed to punish criminals?

    _____

    c. Must God punish all sinners in order to be just and

    righteous? _____

2. **Romans 5:8** Who did Jesus die for? _____.

    a. Was this an act of God's love? _____.

3. **Romans 5:9** By what are we justified? _____.

4. **Romans 1:16** What is God's power that leads to salvation?

_____

5. **2 Thessalonians 1:7-9** Jesus will take vengeance on what two

groups of people? _____

_____

6. **2 Peter 3:9** Does God want anyone to be lost? _____

I responded to His love by . . .

(Find the ultimatum in each passage: "Do _____ or be _____ed.")

1. **Acts 3:22-23** If we do not _____ the Words of Christ we will be _____.

2. **Mark 16:15-16** If we do not _____ and _____ we will be _____.

3. **Luke 13:3** If we do not _____ we will _____

4. **Matthew 10:32-33** If we do not _____ Christ before men He will _____ us before God.

5. **John 3:3-5** If we are not _____ (born of water an spirit) we will not _____ the Kingdom of God.
   a. Can you be saved without being baptized? _____.

6. **1 Corinthians 9:27** If we do not remain faithful to Christ we will be _____.

7. **Revelation 2:10** How long must we be faithful to Christ? _____

The Blessings of being a Christian

1. **1 Peter 3:21** What saved you? _____

2. **Acts 22:16** What did baptism do to your sins? _____
   _____

3. **Galatians 3:27** Baptism put me into _____.

4. **Ephesians 1:3** How many spiritual blessings are found in Christ? _____

    a. How many spiritual blessings are found outside of Christ?

    _____

4. **Ephesians 1:7** In Christ we have _____ through His blood, and _____ of sins through His grace.

5. **Romans 8:1** Is there any condemnation to those who are in Christ? _____

6. **Romans 8:39** Where is the love of God found? _____

7. **2 Timothy 2:1** Where is God's grace found? _____

8. **2 Timothy 2:10** Where is salvation found? _____

9. **1 John 5:11** Where is eternal life found? _____

What else does this mean?

1. **John 3:5** Baptism put me into God's _____.

2. **1 Corinthians 12:13** We are all baptized into _____

3. **Ephesians 1:22-23** Is Jesus the head over **all** things to the Church? _____

   a. The Church is also called _____

   Therefore, baptism put me into the Lord's _____

4. **Ephesians 5:23** Christ is the savior of ____ _____.

   Can anybody be saved outside of the Church (body)? _____

5. **Ephesians 4:4** How many spirits are there? _____

   a. How many hopes do we have? _____

   b. How many Churches (body) are there? _____

6. **Ephesians 5:26** Who sanctifies the Church? _____

   a. How? _____

   b. What is the washing of water? _____

7. **1 Corinthians 6:9-11** When does a person become sanctified and justified before God? _____

8. **Hebrews 10:22** We draw near to God by:

   a. Having a true heart; what does this mean? _____

   b. In full assurance of _____

   c. Having our heart sprinkled from an _____

   (Repenting of our former sinful life).

   d. Having our bodies washed with pure water. What does this mean? _____

Baptism Mark 16:16
Confess Romans 10:9-10
Repent Luke 13:3
Believe John 8:24
Hear John 6:45

Used by permission: World Video Bible School

What does being a Christian require of me?

1. **Colossians 3:1-3** As Christians, we are to seek things that are

   _____, not _____.

2. **Galatians 2:20** Who did Jesus give His life for? _____

   _____

   a. As Christians do we still live for ourselves? _____

   b. Who do we live for? _____

3. Baptism is like an oath or a commitment to live for Christ and no longer for yourself. It is not until one comes up out of the waters of baptism that they are saved, but upon coming out of the water you have now committed your life to Christ.

4. **Revelation 2:10** How long must you be faithful in order to reach Heaven? _____

5. How long do you intend to be faithful to Christ? _____

_____

Summary

God loves me so much that He sent Jesus to die in my place.
I responded to God's love by being baptized into Christ.
My baptism:

> Put me into Christ's Church
>
> Put me into Christ's Kingdom
>
> Put me into Christ's Body
>
> Washed away my sins
>
> Saved me
>
> Sanctified me

Was a commitment to live my life for Christ from this point forward.

Lesson 5
Christian Living

Am I Saved by Grace?

1. Romans 3:24 Are we justified by grace? _____

2. Titus 2:11 What does God's grace bring? _____

    a. To whom has God made that grace available? _____

_____

3. Hebrews 2:9 What enabled Jesus to taste death in our stead?

_____

4. 2 Timothy 2:1 Where is God's grace found? _____

    a. Is there any grace available outside of Christ? _____

Salvation cannot be earned

1. Ephesians 2:8-10 Salvation through faith is a gift from _____

_____

    a. Can it be earned by good works? _____

2. Galatians 2:16 Is it possible to be justified by good works? _

_____

3. James 2:10 Is it possible to keep the law perfectly, so as to earn salvation apart from grace? _____

Salvation must be accepted and maintained

1. John 1:12 Can you be saved if you do not receive Christ? ____

2. Acts 10:34-35 In order to be accepted by God we must:

_____ and _____

3. Revelation 22:17 Will Jesus save any who will not come to Him?

_____

4. Hebrews 5:8-9 Jesus will save only those that _____

5. Galatians 5:4 Once saved is it possible to fall from grace? _

_____

6. Romans 11:22 Must we do something in order to maintain our salvation? _____

    a. What would happen if you didn't? _____

What about faith and works?

1. Romans 10:17 How is faith produced? _____

2. Hebrews 11:6 Is it possible to please God without faith? __

_____

3. James 2:18 Can you demonstrate faith in Christ without good works? _____

4. James 2:19 Do the devils believe in Christ? _____

    a. Will they be saved by that faith? _____

5. James 2:17,24 Can you be saved by faith alone, without doing any good works? _____

What are "good works"?

1. Ephesians 2:8-10 As Christians, God created us anew unto what purpose? _____

    a. Was it God's plan that we should live a life of good works?

    _____

2. Matthew 7:21-23 Did these people think that they were doing good works? _____

    a. What kind of works did Jesus say they were practicing?

    _____

    b. Jesus said good works is doing _____

3. 2 Timothy 3:16-17 What equips us to do good works? _____

_____

4. James 1:27 Pure religion is to care for the _____ and

_____ and to keep yourself

_____.

5. 2 Peter 1:5-9 Is a Christian expected to instantly exhibit all of these qualities? _____

    a. If a Christian fails to cultivate these qualities, what has he

      forgotten? _____

    b. If a Christian develops these qualities will he be unfruitful

      (lacking in good works)? _____

6. Galatians 5:16-25 Can a Christian continue doing the works of the flesh and go to heaven? _____

a. If we have committed to Christ will we seek to crucify (put to death) our desire to do these things? _____

b. If we are actively seeking to live a Christ-like life (walking in the spirit) will we be likely to fulfill the lust of the flesh?

_____

How should I live as a Christian?

1. Colossians 3:17 Everything that we _____ and everything that we _____ should be guided by the authority of _____.

2. 1 Corinthians 11:1 Should we imitate Christ in the way that we live? _____

Should you live in such a way that others could imitate you and be pleasing to God? _____

3. 1 John 1:6-7 Do we have fellowship with God is we do not live our everyday life based on His Word? _____

Moral Issues

1. 2 Peter 1:3 Does the New Testament give us everything that we need to be able to live life acceptably before God? _____

2. John 12:48 By what standard will we be judged on the last day?

_____

a. By what standard should we judge **ALL** moral decisions?

_____

3. Romans 12:9 Should a Christian enjoy taking part in, watching, or listening to anything that is evil or sinful? _____

4. 1 Thessalonians 5:22 A Christian must completely abstain from every _____ of evil.

5. 2 Timothy 2:22 Should a Christian linger in thought over a temptation to sin? _____

6. Matthew 26:41 One effective way to avoid temptation or to deal with it when it arises is to _____

7. 1 Corinthians 15:33 Is it more difficult to remain pure among sinful friends? _____

8. 1 Peter 2:11-12 Should a Christian take part in an activity that could take away from his or her godly influence or might make them less credible in sharing the Gospel? _____

9. Romans 14:23 Is it sin for a Christian to do something that they think _might_ be wrong, even if it is not inherently evil? _____

10. Romans 14:21 Should a Christian do something that might cause others who see their actions to sin, even if it might otherwise be okay? _____

11. 1 Corinthians 6:19-20 Does it glorify God for a Christian to do things that are harmful to his body? _____

    a. If doing such things potentially shortens the useful life of a Christian in God's service, is that wise use of God's blessings? _____

The Christian and Recreation

1. 2 Timothy 3:4 What should we give priority to in the use of our time, energy, and money: God or pleasure? _____

    a. Is recreation necessarily wrong? _____

b. Is recreation wrong when it conflicts with our service to God or obedience to His commands? _____

2. Psalm 101:2-3 Can a faithful Christian enjoy movies or music that promote sin and/or place such images and ideals in his mind?

_____

3. Philippians 4:8 Should a Christian make it a point to fill his mind with these things instead of that which is sinful?

_____

4. Proverbs 6:16-19 If God hates these things; can a faithful Christian enjoy them? _____

5. Psalm 19:14 Should a Christian strive to ensure that the things he puts into his mind are pleasing to God? _____

Questions to ask when considering an activity:

Will this activity bother my conscience at all?

Will it be harmful to my body?

Will it be harmful to me spiritually, or will it threaten my Christian identity?

Will it draw me into associations with a corrupting influence?

Will it make it harder for me to fulfill my commitment to Christ?

Will it weaken my influence on others, or cause others to stumble?

Will it cultivate a fleshly appetite or make me more vulnerable to temptation?

How can I know if I am "growing"?

1. 1 Peter 2:2 What must you desire and use if you are going to grow as a Christian? _____

2. 2 Peter 3:18 Are we commanded to grow as Christians? ____

    a. If you do not increase your knowledge of the Word can you grow as a Christian? _____

Attendance

1. Hebrews 10:24-25 Are we commanded not to miss the services of the Church? _____

2. Matthew 6:33 Is there anything else that could be more important to the faithful Christian? _____

3. Psalm 122:1 Will a faithful Christian attend worship or Bible class out of a sense of obligation, or because he wants to? _____

4. Hebrews 13:17 Are we commanded to obey our elders (so long as their instructions do not conflict with Scripture)? _____

    a. If the elders of your congregation request your presence for a period of study or worship, is it sinful to disregard their request? _____

Personal Study

1. 2 Timothy 2:15 Are we commanded to study the Bible? ____

    a. Can you be approved by God without study? _____

2. Acts 17:11 Should you accept Biblical teaching as fact without verifying it in the Bible for yourself? _____

Prayer

1. 1 Thessalonians 5:17 How often should a Christian pray?

_____

2. Philippians 4:6-7 Is there anything in life that a Christian should not pray about? _____

Thought: Any healthy relationship requires communication. God communicates with us only through the Word. We communicate with Him only through prayer. If you talked and listened to your family as often and about as much as you do with God, would you have a healthy family?

Giving

1. 1 Corinthians 16:1-2 Are we commanded to give in direct proportion to how much we earn? _____

2. 2 Corinthians 9:6-9 Should you give from obligation or with joy out of your love for Christ? _____

3. 2 Corinthians 8:5 If you first give yourself to Christ, would it be easier to give your material blessings to Him? _____

Thought: If your spending habits are a sign of your priorities, what would your bank statement show to be most important in your life?

Summary

Salvation comes by God's grace
> We obtain that grace through an obedient faith.
> We maintain that salvation by living faithfully.

A true Biblical faith is one that works.

Christianity is a lifestyle, not just a hobby.
> It affects all of our moral decisions.
> It affects the activities in which we participate.

A Christian can monitor his spiritual health by watching certain "barometers" in his spiritual life and his relationship with God.

Lesson 6
The Second Law of Pardon

Can I fall away?

1. Hebrews 3:12-13 Can a Christian depart from God? _____

    a. What can cause a Christian to depart? _____

2. 1 Corinthians 10:12 Can a Christian fall? _____

3. 2 Peter 2:20-22 Can a Christian be overcome by sin? _____

4. Romans 11:21-22 What will happen if you do not remain

faithful to Christ? _____

What causes it?

1. 2 Peter 2:1 Will there be false teachers in the Church? _____

    a. What happens to those who follow these false teachers?

_____

2. 2 Peter 3:16 Can the Scriptures be twisted and misused? ____

a. What happens when we do that? _____

3. Matthew 13:21 Can persecution or hardship cause a Christian to fall away if he is not grounded in the faith? _____

4. Luke 8:14 Can the mundane things of life, such as work, or other things that make us busy distract you and cause you to fall away? _____

a. Would such a departure be sudden, or gradual and hard to notice? _____

5. 1 John 2:15-17 Satan had three types of temptation that can cause is to fall away; what are they?

a. _____

b. _____

c. _____

How do I prevent it?

1. 1 Timothy 4:16 What two things should you watch closely to ensure your own salvation?

a. _____

b. _____

2. 1 Corinthians 9:27 Should you constantly work to keep your body and the way you use it under control? _____

a. What could happen if you don't? _____

3. 2 Peter 1:5-10 If you are actively doing these things are you likely to fall away? _____

a. What if you don't do these things? _____

b. Can you be certain of your soul's condition? _____

4. Hebrews 5:12-14 Is a Christian expected to grow in the faith?

_____

    a. How does this growth take place? _____

    b. What is the result of this growth? _____

How do I know if something is okay?
What's the standard?

1. John 12:48 What standard will judge us? _____

2. Psalm 119:11 What standard can keep us from sin? _____

_____

    a. Can God's Word help you if you don't know it? _____

Is my conscience a safe guide?

1. Acts 23:1 Was Paul sinning when he killed Christians? _____

    a. Did he still have a good conscience? _____

    b. Does a good conscience necessarily mean you are not in
sin? _____

2. 1 Corinthians 8:7 Does everybody's conscience have proper
knowledge of right and wrong according to Scripture? _____

    a. IF your conscience **does** have proper knowledge of right
and wrong according to Scripture can it keep you from sin?

_____

3. Romans 14:23 Is it a sin to do something that bothers your
conscience, even if the Bible does not say that thing is a sin? __

_____

What about my example?

1. Colossians 4:5-6 Should a Christian be thoughtful about how his actions influence others? _____

2. 1 Corinthians 8:10-13 Is it a sin to act in such a way that you cause others to sin, even if your actions are not necessarily wrong?

_____

How do I Overcome Sin?

1. John 16:33 Has Jesus already overcome the world? _____

2. John 15:4,10 If we keep Christ's commandments do we abide in Him? _____

    a. If we abide in Him does He abide in us? _____

3. 1 John 4:4 If Christ abides in us can we overcome sin (the world)? _____

Understanding Temptation

1. Hebrews 4:15 Was Jesus tempted? _____

    a. Did Jesus sin? _____

    b. Is it a sin to be tempted? _____

2. James 1:12-16 Does God tempt us to sin? _____

    a. What draws us away? _____

    b. When Satan gives us an opportunity (entices us) to act on that desire, this is when we are tempted.

    c. What happens when we act on that desire? _____

    d. What is the result of that sin? _____

e. Can we keep from giving in? _____

Desire + Opportunity = Temptation

Temptation + Action = Sin

Sin = Death

f. If you control your desire will you sin? _____

g. If you cannot control your desire, but limit your opportunity will you sin? _____

h. If you cannot control your desire or opportunity, but control your action will you sin? _____

What are our weapons?

1. Romans 12:21 With what are we to overcome evil? _____

2. 1 John 5:4 What is it that helps us to overcome the world?

_____

3. John 8:51 Will you fall away if you keep Christ's Words? ____

4. Ephesians 6:11-18 If you put on the whole armor of God can you withstand temptation? _____

a. Even with all of this armor must you actively stand against temptation to avoid falling? _____

b. v. 14 Is truth the very foundation of our defense? __

c. v. 14 The next component of our arsenal is: _____

d. Can a Christian avoid falling without living a righteous life? _____

e. v. 15 What protects us as we walk through life? _____

f. Is the Gospel an effective protection without constant preparation and study? _____

g. v. 16 What will help you sustain fiery trials and temptations? _____

h. v. 17 What protects you from a fatal blow (head)?

_____

i. (Acts 4:12) Where is the only place to find this protection? _____

j. v. 17 What is your only offensive weapon? _____

_____

k. v. 18 What activity keeps your guard vigilant? _____

_____

When I sin, how can I be restored?

1. Acts 8:13 Did Simon become a Christian through Gospel obedience? _____

2. Acts 8:18-21 Did Simon sin by bribing Peter? _____

    a. Was he lost again at this point? _____

3. Acts 8:22-24 Peter told Simon to do two things to be restored. What were they? _____

4. 2 Corinthians 7:9-11 Is repentance more than feeling sorry?

_____

    a. Does repentance involve clearing yourself of the sin?

    _____

    b. Does repentance involve a resolve to do well? _____

5. 1 John 1:6-10 Can you have fellowship with God if there is sin that you have not dealt with? _____

    a. If you fail to confess sin will it be forgiven? _____

    b. Will God "forget" about it over time? _____

    c. If you repent, confess your sin, and pray for forgiveness will it be forgiven? _____

When do I have to confess and to whom?

1. Matthew 18:15-17 If you have sinned against only one person (other than God), and only you and that person know, do you need to confess your sin to that person as well as to God?

_____

    a. Do you need to confess that sin to anybody else? ____

2. Revelation 2:23 If you have sinned and nobody else knows about it does God still know? _____

    a. Do you need to confess that sin to God in prayer? __

    b. Do you need to confess that sin to anybody else? __

3. James 5:16 If your sin is publicly known, or you don't know how many people know (forsaking the assembly, a private sin that has spread through gossip, etc) should you confess that sin to the Church? _____

    a. Can that sin be forgiven otherwise? _____

    b. Such confession can be made by: responding to the invitation, asking an elder or preacher to announce your repentance, or having a statement placed in the bulletin.

4. 1 John 1:7 As Christians if we obey the second law of pardon does Jesus' blood continue to cleanse all of our sins? _____

    a. Does Jesus' blood continue to cleanse our sins if we do not? _____

Summary

A Christian can fall from grace and be lost.
> False teachers can lead us away.
> We can twist the Scriptures.
> We can become discouraged through hardships.
> We can get caught up in the mundane things of life
> We can be drawn away by sin.

Apostasy can be prevented.
> We must watch ourselves.
> We must watch our doctrine.
> We must continue to grow and mature as Christians.

We must use the Bible as our standard of conduct and teaching.

We can overcome sin and temptation
> By controlling our desire
> By controlling our opportunities
> By controlling our actions
> By using the tools God gave us

When we fall into sin we can be restored by:
> Repentance
> Confession
> Prayer

Lesson 7
About the Bible

Do I need anything else?

1. 2 Peter 1:3 Had God revealed everything that we need to know before the apostles died? _____

2. 1 John 1:3-4 Did the apostles write down everything God revealed to them? _____

    a. Do their writings give us everything that we need to have fellowship with God? _____

3. Jude 3 Since the Gospel was delivered once and for all time during the first century, does God need to speak to people today?

_____

4. Galatians 1:6-9 If an angel were to speak to you today, would that angel be sent by God? _____

a. If an apostle or prophet were to speak to you today, would that messenger be sent by God? _____

Is it all-authoritative?

1. Matthew 28:18 Who has all authority today? _____

2. Hebrews 1:1-2 Who is the only authorized spokesman of God until the end of time? _____

3. John 14:26 Did the Holy Spirit ensure that the all-authoritative words of Jesus would be preserved in the Bible?

_____

4. John 12:48 Will all people be judged by the all-authoritative words of Christ? _____

a. Will we be judged by any other standard such as: Opinions, beliefs, feelings, the Church, elders, preachers, teachers, family, friends, religious creeds, catechisms, counsels, synods? _____

Is it all-sufficient?

1. 2 Timothy 3:15-17 What source teaches you about salvation?

_____

a. Are the Scriptures able to make you complete before God?

_____

b. Is there any good work that God might require which the Scriptures do not prepare you for? _____

2. 2 Peter 1:3 Do the Scriptures give you everything that you need to know to live a successful life? _____

a. Do the Scriptures give you everything you need to know to be godly? _____

b. Do you need anything other than the Bible to guide you spiritually? _____

c. Since the Scriptures are all-sufficient, do you need any type of miraculous or supernatural guidance from Heaven?

_____

d. Since the Scriptures are all-sufficient, do you need any other books, the Church, or people to tell you what it means?

_____

What is binding today (and what's not)?[1]

1. Matthew 16:18-19 Did Jesus command the apostles to bind (command) and loose (allow) only those things that God (heaven) had already commanded or allowed? _____

a. Did Jesus tell the apostles that what they taught would be authoritative? _____

2. 1 Thessalonians 2:13 How are we to receive the things that the apostles taught? _____

---

[1] This section relies heavily on <u>When Is a Bible Example Binding</u> by Thomas Warren.

3. 2 Thessalonians 3:6 Does God accept those who do not live in accordance with what the apostles taught? _____

How do you establish authority?

1. 1 Thessalonians 5:21 Is every teaching or idea that you might hear going to be good? _____

> **a.** What are you to do with teachings or ideas that are not good? _____

2. Acts 17:11 How can you determine what teachings or ideas must be followed and which must be rejected? _____

> **a.** Does this require you to reason logically with Scripture? -
>
> _____

FACT

In order to determine if a Biblical instruction or teaching is binding upon us today we must:

> 1. **Carefully analyze the statement under consideration**
> 2. **Carefully analyze the entire context of the passage**
> 3. **Draw *only* those conclusions that the evidence supports.**

Is an Old Testament example binding?

1. Colossians 2:14 Are *any* of the commands in the Old Testament (without being repeated in the New Testament) binding on us today? _____

2. Romans 15:4 Why is the Old Testament record still preserved?

_____

a. Then, are the *principles* seen in the Old Testament still applicable today? _____

3. 1 Corinthians 10:6, 11 Does God expect us to learn from the examples set forth in the Old Testament? _____

a. Does God expect us to apply the principles we learn from those examples? _____

Is a New Testament example binding?

1. 1 Peter 2:21 Are we commanded to try to follow the example of Christ in our lives today? _____

2. 1 Corinthians 11:1 Are we commanded to try to follow the example of Paul (insomuch that he followed Christ) in our lives today? _____

3. Philippians 3:17 Are we commanded to follow the example of other New Testament Christians (insomuch as they followed Christ)? _____

FACT

There are five types of actions found in the New Testament:

Permanently Sinful (Peter's denial of Christ)

Optional & Temporary(Things we can no longer do today)

Optional & Permanent (Things that are value-neutral)

Obligatory & Temporary (Proper use of miraculous gifts)

Obligatory & Permanent (Baptism, Lord's Supper)

Through the proper use of reason we can determine what examples we must follow, and which we must not.

EXAMPLE

4. Acts 20:7 What was the Church's purpose for coming together?

_____

5. 1 Corinthians 11:26 How long must we continue to follow this example? _____

    a. On what day of the week did the first century Church do this? _____

    b. Did they do this every week? _____

    c. Did they do this on any other day of the week? _____

    d. Were their actions acceptable to God? _____

    e. If we followed their example would we be acceptable to God? _____

    f. Does the New Testament authorize any deviation from this example? _____

Is the Bible really God's Word?

How did it get here?

1. Acts 10:36 How did God speak to His people? _____

2. John 15:26-27 Who revealed Jesus' Word to the apostles?

_____

    a. What did the apostles do with Jesus' Word? _____

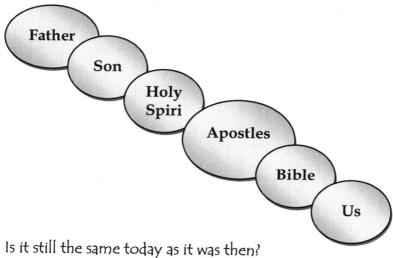

Is it still the same today as it was then?

1. Matthew 24:35 Did Jesus promise that the Bible would be preserved for all time? _____

    a. Is God powerful enough to keep that promise? _____

2. Hebrews 13:8 Does Jesus ever change? _____

    a. Would He break His promise? _____

<u>FACT:</u> The oldest Bible manuscripts in existence today date from around 350-400 AD.

Homer wrote <u>the Odyssey</u> roughly 1,000 years before Christ; yet the oldest manuscript of his work dates to roughly 1,000 years *after* Christ.

There are over 5,000 ancient manuscripts of the Bible in existence today.

Any errors made in one of these manuscripts would not be very likely to have affected all 5,000+ manuscripts.

When faced with a variation in the reading of the text, we simply have to see what the majority supports to find the genuine Biblical text.

What about all these different translations?

1. Revelation 22:18-19 Does God take His Word seriously? ___

    a. Is God pleased if anything is omitted from His Word?

    _____

    b. Is God pleased if anything is added to His Word?

    _____

    c. Is God pleased if any substitutions are made in His Word?

    _____

    d. Does the Bible teach that *every word* which is found in the original text is exactly the word (case and tense included) that God intended? _____

Thought: Since the every word in the Bible was literally "God-breathed." Shouldn't we look for a *word for word* translation?

_____

FACT: There are basically three philosophies of translation:

    1. Word for word translation from the original into English.

    2. Paraphrase – the translator reads the passage, decides what it means, then writes.

    3. "Mix between word for word and thought for thought" – The translator basically translates word for word, then rephrases the sentence how he/she thinks it best makes sense.

2. Which philosophy best fits with the Bible's teaching on inspiration? _____

3. Do the other philosophies fit with the Bibles teaching? _____

FACT The KJV, NKJV, ASV, and ESV are translated word for word.

No other English versions are!

Summary

The Bible is the only source of information that is needed for true Christianity.

> The New Testament is All-authoritative.
> The New Testament is All-sufficient.
> No other communication from God is necessary.

The inspired teaching of the apostles is still binding today.

> We are to receive their teaching as the Word of God.
> We must consider Scripture carefully and reason with it properly to determine what is necessary for Christians today.
> The Old Testament examples teach us principles today.
> The New Testament examples teach us both principles and doctrine today.

Jesus promised to preserve His all-authoritative Word for all time.

> He kept that promise.
> We must do our part by teaching and studying from only those translations that respect the authority and inspiration of Scripture.

Lesson 8
How to Study the Bible

Is Personal Study really necessary?

1. 2 Timothy 2:15 Is Bible study commanded? _____

    a. Can you be approved before God without study? _____

2. Acts 17:10-11 Why were the Bereans commended? _____

_____

    a. How often did they study? _____

    b. Why did they study? _____

3. Hebrews 5:12-14 Does God expect you to grow in your Bible

knowledge? _____

4. 2 Timothy 3:16-17 Does the Bible prepare you for living a

Christian life? _____

    a. Can you be prepared to live a Christian life without studying

the Bible? _____

How Should I Approach my study?

Attitude

1. Habakkuk 2:1 Should we approach Bible study with reverence for the Word of God? _____

2. Ephesians 5:17 Can you understand the Bible? _____

3. Philippians 4:9 Should you approach Bible study looking for ways to be more like Christ? _____

4. Colossians 1:9 Should we approach Bible study with prayer?

_____

Scheduling

1. Matthew 5:6 How often do you eat? _____

   a. What's the longest you've ever been without food? _____

   _____

   b. Is spiritual nourishment more important than food? _____

   c. Should Bible study be a priority in your schedule? _____

"Spare time is better than no time, but the best time is planned time – a time set aside through sheer determination. Then, you will be surprised how much spare time you can add to this." – Russell L. Simmons

2. Choose a time that you can set aside *at least* thirty minutes for Bible study every day: _____

Let nothing interfere with your daily time of study (you wouldn't let anything interfere with your meal times).

Commitment

Bible study has a lot in common with diet and exercise. Most people agree that these are important things to do. A lot of people set out to do them. Very few actually stick to it.

Here are a few things you can do to avoid allowing your personal Bible study to go the way of most New Year's resolutions:

1. If possible, study at the same TIME and PLACE every day.
2. Put your daily study into your schedule.
3. Set reminders for yourself.
4. Find an "accountability partner" that can help you make sure that you keep on track with your study.
    a. Iron sharpeneth iron; so a man sharpeneth the countenance of his friend. Proverbs 27:17
5. Follow a set schedule and plan of study.

Bible Society Survey

16% read something from the Bible every day.
A further 9% read the Bible several times a week.
11% read something from the Bible about once a week.
9% read the Bible about once a month.
16% read the Bible several times a year.
7% had read something from the Bible once in the past year.

14% had not read anything from the Bible in the past year.

A further 18% have never read anything from the Bible at any time in their lives.

Survey conducted by Taylor Nelson AGB, commissioned by Bible Society in May, 1997. 776 people aged 16 or over who attended a Trinitarian Church at least once a month were interviewed face-to-face at home in England and Wales

Purpose

1. Romans 1:16-17 Can you learn about God without studying the Bible? _____

2. Psalm 119:155 Can you learn about salvation without studying the Bible? _____

3. 1 Thessalonians 4:18 Does God's Word provide comfort?

_____

4. Philippians 1:21 Does God's Word provide strength in the face of death? _____

5. Proverbs 19:16 Does God's Word warn us of Hell and tell us how to avoid it? _____

6. 2 Timothy 4:7-8 Does God's Word tell us of Heaven and how we can get there? _____

How do I study effectively?

Organization

1. Study with a notepad and your Bible.

2. Study with a pen or highlighter *in your hand.*

3. Keep the other (pen or highlighter) within reach.

4. Take ownership of your Bible.

    a. Highlight key words or verses.

    b. Make notes in the margin and in the text.

5. Write down:

    a. questions

    b. ideas

    c. thoughts

    d. Points to remember

    e. Scriptures to memorize

6. Outline the text in your notepad.

7. Questions to answer when reading the Bible:
    a. Who?

        i. Is speaking

        ii. Is being spoken to

    b. When was this written?

    c. Where is the writer/readers?

    d. What is being said?

    e. Why is this being said?

    f. How is this being said?

Tools
Bible Translations
1. Translation Philosophies
Word-for-Word:
As much as possible, biblical scholars take each "word" from the original Greek or Hebrew text and an English word in its place.
Thought-for-Thought:
Translators take the "meaning" of the original language and rewrite it in modern language that's easy to read and understand.

Balanced Approach:

Translators use a blend between word-for-word translation and thought for thought where they judge that the text needs clarification, or to try to update an ancient idiom.[2]

2. Choose a translation that respects the Word-for word "God breathed" (2 Timothy 3:16) method of inspiration.

English dictionaries

a. Webster's Dictionary

PROPH'ET, n. [L. propheta.]

1. One that foretells future events; a predicter; a foreteller.
2. In Scripture, a person illuminated, inspired or instructed by God to announce future events; as Moses, Elijah, David, Isaiah, &c.

b. Vine's Complete Expository Dictionary of Old and New Testament Words

PROPH'ET

1. *prophetes*, 4396 "one who speaks forth or openly" (see PROPHECY, A), "A proclaimer of a divine message," denoted among the Greeks an interpreter of the oracles of the gods.

Greek and Hebrew Dictionaries

a. Strong's Hebrew and Greek Dictionaries

H5030

נביא nâbîy' *naw-bee'*

From H5012; a *prophet* or (generally) *inspired* man: - prophecy, that prophesy, prophet.

G4396

---

[2]**http://www.zondervan.com/Cultures/en-US/Product/Bible/Translations/About+Bible+Translations.htm?QueryStringSite=Zondervan**

Προφήτης prophētēs *prof-ay'-tace*

From a compound of <u>G4253</u> and <u>G5346</u>; a *foreteller* ("prophet"); by analogy an *inspired speaker*, by extension a *poet:* - prophet.

b. Thayer's Greek Definitions
G4396

Προφήτης prophētēs
Thayer Definition:

1) in Greek writings, an interpreter of oracles or of other hidden things

Part of Speech: noun masculine

c. Brown-Driver-Brigg's Hebrew Definitions
H5030

נביא nabîy'
BDB Definition:

1) spokesman, speaker, prophet

    1a) prophet

    1b) false prophet

    1c) heathen prophet

Part of Speech: noun masculine

Concordances
Prophet

For he is a p. and he shall pray	Gen 20:7	5030
Aaron thy brother shall be thy p.	Ex 7:1	5030
If there be a p. among you	Num 12:6	5030
If there arise among you a p.	Deut 13:1	5030
Hearken unto the words of that p	Deut 13:3	5030
And that p. or that dreamer of	Deut 13:5	5030
Thee a p. from the midst of thee	Deut 18:15	5030

Strong's Exhaustive Concordance of the Bible

Young's Analytical Concordance to the Bible

Cruden's Complete Concordance to the Old and New Testaments.

With the concordance you can also study all of the teachings of the Bible on any subject. List these Scriptures on a piece of paper and read them in the Bible. Make notes about what God says regarding your selected subject.

References in Your Bible

Cross References

These are usually located between the columns of the text, and have been added by uninspired men. They can be useful to tell you where to find similar or related passages, especially Old Testament verses that are being quoted in the New Testament. They are usually keyed to letters or numbers that appear as a superscript within the Biblical text and are located as close as possible to the verse to which they refer.

These cross references can be useful in doing a deeper study. Simply keep in mind that these connections were made by men. While they are usually correct, sometimes they are not. Some of these references may also contain notes about the meaning of certain words within the text.

Other Helps

Most Bibles also contain introductions, outlines, maps, and other useful helps. These can often be very beneficial to the diligent student. Just remember that they are also man-made, and therefore subject to error. Only the text of the Bible itself is inerrant.

Electronic tools

There are many electronic tools that are now available for your use in Bible study. There are electronic Bibles, commentaries, dictionaries, etc. All of these have been made available as a standalone device, or as software for your computer or PDA. One great resource that is free can be found here:
http://www.e-sword.net/

This software has a lot of tools and helps available for download, both free, and at a price. They include: Bible translations, dictionaries, concordances, commentaries, and maps. Using this software, or another similar program can be a great way to gain access to all of the above mentioned tools at little to no cost, and have them all in one place.

Plan

Your daily study of the Bible should follow a clear, predetermined plan. It should include some memorization. There are several methods from which you can choose:

1. Topical Study
   a. Choose a topic and write down everything that you currently understand about this topic.
   b. Research your chosen topic in a few good Bible dictionaries. Write down what you find.
   c. Look up your chosen topic in a good concordance, or perform a search in your Bible program.
   d. Study each verse that you find and write down what that verse teaches concerning your chosen topic.
   e. Review everything that you have learned and draw a specific logical conclusion as to what the Bible teaches on your chosen topic.
   f. Compare what you have learned to what you knew when you began. Revise your understanding based on what you have learned from the Bible.

2. Word Study

This type of study is performed in the same way as a topical study, but it is looking at one specific word, such as "baptism."

3. Character Study

   a. Choose a person in the Bible to study. Write down everything that you know about that person.
   b. Using a good concordance, find every passage that speaks about that person. Write down the verses.
   c. Read every passage that you found. Also read the section of verses before and after each passage so that you can understand the context of your passage.
   d. Make notes of what you learn about this person, how God dealt with them, and how they reacted to God.
   e. Draw specific conclusions about what you can learn and how you can apply these lessons to your life.

4. Textual Study

   a. This is the most fundamental method of study. This method can take you through the entire Bible cover to cover, and build a foundation of knowledge for your faith.
   b. This can be done by:
      1. Studying straight through the Bible
      2. Studying through the Bible Chronologically.
      3. Studying through a book of the Bible.
      4. Studying through any given section of Scripture.
   c. First answer the six questions listed above as they pertain to the selected text. Then read through the text, making notes of what you find. Also make specific applications to your life.

What do I need to know first?

The **purpose** of the Bible is to glorify God, to teach us about Him, and how we can have a relationship with Him.

The **theme** of the Bible is "**Christ is coming**." The Old Testament says "Christ is coming." The New Testament says "Christ is coming back."

History

The Bible gives the history of God's dealings with man. It can be divided into three historical "dispensations," or laws that were given to man by God.

1. **Patriarchal Dispensation** This is God's dealings with all of mankind through the male head of each family, from the beginning of time until the giving of the Law of Moses at Mount Sinai. God continued to deal with the Gentiles in this manner until the Cross.

2. **Mosaic Dispensation** This is God's dealing with the Jews through the Law of Moses. This lasts from Mount Sinai (Exodus 20) to the Cross.

3. **Christian Dispensation** This is God's dealing with all mankind from the day of Pentecost (Acts 2) until the end of time. We all live under this Law, which is recorded in the New Testament, today.

Divisions

I. Old Testament (39 books)
   A. Law (5 books)
   B. History (12 books)
   C. Poetry (5 books)
   D. Prophets (17 books)

II. New Testament (27 books)
   A. Gospel accounts (4 books)
   B. History (Acts)
   C. Epistles (21 books)
   D. Prophecy (Revelation)

III. Memorize
   A. These divisions
   B. The names of each book in the New Testament
   C. The names of each book in the Old Testament

Summary

Personal Bible Study is important.
     Because it is commanded
     To be approved before God
     To make sure you are learning the truth
     To grow as a Christian
     To be prepared for life as a Christian
Personal Bible Study should be approached
     With a proper attitude
     With a firm schedule
     With commitment
     With Purpose
     With Prayer
Effective Bible study is:
     Organized
     Is helped by the proper use of tools:
          Dictionaries
          Concordances
          Bible References and helps
          Electronic Tools
     Follows a plan
Personal Bible Study should be done with a proper understanding of the organization of Scripture.

Lesson 9
Worship in the Assembly

Is Assembling for Worship important?

1. Hebrews 10:23-25 Can a Christian regularly miss the services of the Church without wavering in his faith?

_____

  a. Does assembling for worship help prepare us for Christ's return? _____

  b. Should we assemble for worship to encourage other Christians in the Faith? _____

2. Luke 4:16 Did Jesus make a habit of worshipping God regularly? _____

  a. Would Jesus miss a service of the Church? _____

3. Hebrews 13:17 Are we commanded to submit to our elders?

_____

    a. If the elders ask the congregation to assemble two or three times per week are we obligated to do so? _____

    b. Is it a sin not to submit to the elders in this request? _____

4. Hebrews 13:15 Are we commanded to praise God through worship? _____

    a. Is this the proper way to show our thanks for His love? ___

How are we to worship?

1. John 4:23-24 How must we worship God? _____

_____

    a. Can our worship be acceptable if it is not sincere? _____

2. Matthew 15:9 Is our worship acceptable if it is based on the commandments of men? _____

3. Leviticus 10:1-2 God had commanded them to use fire from the altar (Lev 16:12). He had not said anything about *not* using other fire. His specific command eliminated all other options.

    a. Can we add to or change the pattern of worship given in the New Testament and be pleasing to God? _____

_____

The Lord's Supper

1. Luke 22:17-20 What does the bread represent? _____

_____

    a. What does the grape juice represent? _____

_____

    b. Why did Jesus say to do this? _____

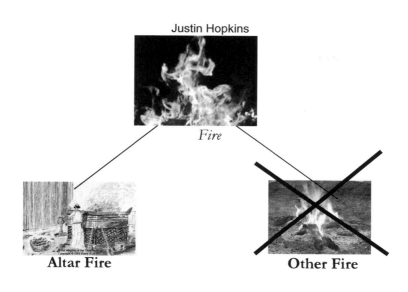

Justin Hopkins

Fire

Altar Fire   **Other Fire**

_____

2. 1 Corinthians 11:23-29 What does the Lord's Supper symbolize?

_____

  a. How long are we to continue this practice? _____

    _____

  b. What happens if you do this in an unworthy manner?

    _____

  c. Are we commanded to examine our own lives when we

  observe this memorial? _____

3. Acts 20:7 When did Christians observe the Lord's Supper?

_____

    a. Did they do this every week? _____

    b. Should we do this every week? _____

    c. When should we stop doing this? _____

Giving

1. 1 Corinthians 16:1-2 When did Paul command us to give?

_____

    a. Is our giving to be done based on how much we have been

    blessed? _____

2. 2 Corinthians 9:6-8 Should you plan in advance how much you

are going to give? _____

    a. What kind of giver does God love? _____

    b. Can you give so much that God is unable to bless you

    enough to sustain you? _____

3. 2 Corinthians 8:1-5 In their deep poverty, how did these

Christians give? _____

    a. What did they give to the Lord first? _____

    b. If you were to give yourself to God first, how would that

    effect your giving? _____

4. Luke 21:1-4 Was Jesus watching how much these people gave?

_____

    a. Did He care more about how much they gave or _how_ they

    gave? _____

    b. Does Jesus watch when we give today? _____

Singing

1. Ephesians 5:18-20 When we sing, who are we speaking to?

_____

a. If we are speaking to ourselves, are we speaking to those who are not singing with us? _____

b. What instrument does God command us to use to make melody? _____

2. Colossians 3:16 Who are we teaching when we sing? _____

_____

a. If we are teaching ourselves, are we speaking to those who are not singing with us? _____

b. Who is our praise and thanksgiving directed to? _____

3. 1 Corinthians 14:15 When we sing are we to sing with our emotions to the Lord? _____

a. When we sing are we to understand what we are singing?

_____

b. Is it acceptable to sing a song that teaches something that does not agree with Scripture? _____

c. Is it acceptable to sing a song in a worship setting that neither praises God nor teaches spiritual truths? _____

d. Is it acceptable to add mechanical instruments to our singing, since they are not mentioned in the specific command? _____

Teaching & Preaching

1. Acts 2:42 What is the first thing that Luke mentions the Christians continuing to do? _____

2. Acts 20:7 Who was gathered together? _____

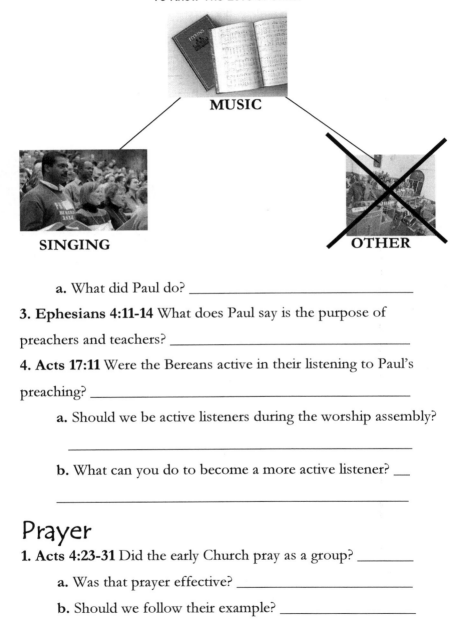

MUSIC

SINGING   **OTHER**

    a. What did Paul do? _____

3. Ephesians 4:11-14 What does Paul say is the purpose of

preachers and teachers? _____

4. Acts 17:11 Were the Bereans active in their listening to Paul's

preaching? _____

    a. Should we be active listeners during the worship assembly?

    _____

    b. What can you do to become a more active listener? ___

    _____

Prayer

1. Acts 4:23-31 Did the early Church pray as a group? _____

    a. Was that prayer effective? _____

    b. Should we follow their example? _____

2. 1 Corinthians 14:14-17 Is it important that the public prayer is understood by all? _____

Who can lead in Worship?

1. 1 Timothy 2:8-14 Who does Paul say should lead public prayer?

_____

    a. Is a woman allowed to teach or take a role with authority when the Church is assembled? _____

    b. Why/why not? _____

_____

    c. Is this reason cultural, or a universal heritage for all of mankind? _____

2. 1 Corinthians 14:34-35 Is it proper for women to ask questions or to speak when the Church is assembled to worship?

_____

3. Titus 2:1-5 Who is a woman permitted to teach in a public setting? _____

4. Acts 18:24-26 Was Priscilla involved in teaching the Gospel to Apollos? _____

    a. Can a Christian woman teach the Gospel to a non-Christian man in a private study? _____

5. 1 Corinthians 14:40 Should order and a reverent solemnity prevail during a worship service? _____

Summary

Assembling for worship is important.

     Because it is commanded

     To build one another up

     To submit to the elders

     To grow as a Christian

     To glorify God!

The Lord's Supper

     Is a time to reflect on Christ's sacrifice

     Is a time to examine your own life

Giving of your means

     Is commanded

     Is a free-will offering to God

     Is to be in direct proportion to your blessings

Singing

     Is to be done by everybody

     Must teach sound doctrine

     Is to be done with your heart & mind

Teaching & Preaching

     Is an act of worship

     Is something in which we must ALL be active

Public Prayer

     Is a time that we can go to God as a family

     Is to be done with meaning

Lesson 10
Teach Us How to Pray

Does God Answer My Prayers?
Who does God hear?

1. Isaiah 59:1-2 Does God hear the prayers of those living in sin?

_____

2. John 9:31 Does God hear the sinner's prayer? _____

3. 1 Peter 3:12 Whose prayer does God listen to? _____

What can hinder my prayer?

1. 1 Peter 3:7 Can your marriage relationship affect your

relationship with God? _____

2. Matthew 6:5-8 If your purpose in prayer is to look righteous to others is your prayer heard by God? _____

    a. If your prayer is a meaningless script that you quote is it heard by God? _____

3. Matthew 6:14-15 If you fail to forgive others will your prayers be heard by God? _____

4. Luke 18:9-14 If you pray with a self-righteous attitude is your prayer head by God? _____

5. James 4:3 If you pray with a selfish attitude and motivation will your prayer be heard by God? _____

Does Prayer change things?

1. Matthew 7:7-11 Will God bless those that come to Him in proper manner? _____

    a. Will our heavenly Father deal with our requests at least as justly as an earthly father would? _____

2. James 5:16-18 Is the sincere prayer of a faithful Christian effective? _____

    a. What happened when Elijah prayed? _____

    b. Is the prayer of a faithful Christian just as effective as his was? _____

3. 2 Kings 20:1-7 Was Hezekiah's prayer heard by God? _____

    a. Was his prayer able to change God's mind? _____

    b. Can our prayers be just as effective with God? _____

How Should I Pray?

1. Luke 6:12 Was prayer an important part of Jesus' life? _____

    a. Did He set an example of prayer for us to follow? ___

2. Luke 11:1 Did John the immerser see prayer as being important?

_____

    a. Did He teach his disciples how to properly pray to God?

    _____

    b. Can you maintain a good relationship with God without

    speaking to Him? _____

    c. Can you speak to God without prayer? _____

    d. Should we also desire to be taught how to pray? _____

What is the proper attitude?

1. James 1:5-7 When you pray to God, must you pray in faith?

_____

    a. Will God hear your prayer if you doubt that He will?

    _____

    b. Will God answer your prayer if you doubt that He will?

    _____

2. Matthew 21:22 If you pray with a belief that your prayer will be

heard, will it be answered? _____

3. 1 Corinthians 14:15 When you pray, should your prayer be filled

with meaning and emotion (spirit)? _____

    a. Should your prayer be one that is thought out and

    purposeful? _____

What is the proper preparation?

1. 1 Peter 3:12 How must you live if your prayer is to be heard?

_____

2. John 15:7 What condition does Jesus place on our prayers being answered? _____

3. 1 John 3:22 How can you know that your prayer will be heard?

_____

4. Proverbs 28:9 If you fail to obediently hear God's Word will He hear you? _____

5. Matthew 6:14-15 Will God hear your prayer if you have failed to forgive another? _____

What is the proper position?

1. Luke 22:41 What position did Jesus assume here to pray?

_____

    a. Was His prayer acceptable? _____

2. Luke 18:13-14 What position did the publican assume to pray?

_____

    a. Was his prayer acceptable? _____

3. Matthew 26:39 What position did Jesus assume here to pray?

_____

    a. Was His prayer acceptable? _____

4. Luke 24:30 What position did Jesus assume here to pray?

_____

    a. Was His prayer acceptable? _____

"The Bible does not tell us what physical position to assume when praying. In Bible times, the Jews normally stood with *outstretched* hands [1 Timothy 2:8] However, God-fearing men assumed other positions as well. It is the condition of the heart, and not the position of the body that is important in prayer."[3]

What is the proper place?

1. 1 Timothy 2:8 Where does Paul say we are to pray?

_____

    a. Is there any place that we cannot pray? _____

What is the proper time?

1. 1 Thessalonians 5:17 When does Paul command us to pray?

_____

    a. Is there any time that you should not pray? _____

2. Luke 18:1 How often does Jesus say we ought to pray?

_____

    a. Should you ever grow weary of praying? _____

What is the proper form?

1. Matthew 6:9 To whom does Jesus say our prayers should be

directed? _____

---

[3] (Bobby Bates, 1988)

"In every instance when an inspired person talks about prayer, God, the Father is the one to whom we must direct our prayers/ No inspired person ever instructs anyone to pray to Jesus, the Holy Spirit, angels, "saints," departed spirits, or anyone else."[4]

2. John 16:23-24 In who's name are we to pray to the Father?

_____

3. Ephesians 2:18 We have access to God through whom?

_____

    a. Can our prayers reach God any other way? _____

4. Romans 8:34 Who intercedes (acts as the mediator, or go-between) between us and God? _____

5. 1 John 5:14-15 Is a prayer acceptable if we ask for something that is against the will of God? _____

    a. Should all prayers be offered with the understanding and desire for God's Will to be done above all else?

    _____

6. Matthew 6:13 What word does Jesus use to conclude the model prayer? _____

This word occurs roughly 30 times in the Old Testament and 152 in the New. Jesus used it regularly to emphasize the truth or certainty of a statement (Matthew 6:16 "verily"). It carries the idea

---

[4] Ibid

of certainty or faithfulness. "So used in our prayers ought to express certainty and assurance in the Lord to whom we pray."[5]

"It was a custom, which passed from the synagogues into the Christian assemblies, that when he who had read or discoursed had offered up a solemn prayer to God, the others in attendance responded *Amen*, and thus made the substance of what was uttered their own."[6]

    a. Should we understand and fully agree with a prayer, or

saying in a sermon before we say "amen?" _____

How we communicate with God:

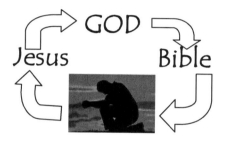

For What Should I Pray?

1. Romans 8:26-27 If you do not know how to express your

thoughts and feelings in prayer, does God still know and

understand what you are trying to say? _____

---

[5] (Theological Wordbook of the Old Testament, 1980)

[6] (Joseph Henry Thayer, 1889)

The Model Prayer (Matthew 6:9-13)

1. Did Jesus command us to pray this specific prayer, or to pray in a similar manner? _____

I.   Address – prayer is directed to God (v. 9)

II.   Praise – Giving praise to the God of Heaven and earth (v. 9)

III. Petition – Asking God for blessings, for Him, others, and yourself (v. 10-11)

IV. Confession – Confession of sins and a petition for forgiveness (v. 12-13). See also 1 John 1:9

V.   Closing – Traditionally it is here that an appeal to the name & authority of Christ is made "in Jesus name" (v. 13)

Thanksgiving

1. Colossians 4:2 Are we commanded to include the giving of thanks in our prayers to God? _____

2. Romans 1:21 Are we pleasing to God if we fail to be thankful and express our gratitude toward Him? _____

Intercession

1. Timothy 2:1-4 Are we commanded to offer up prayers on behalf of other people? _____

   a. Can others be saved by your prayers, or must they still come to an obedient knowledge of the truth? _____

2. 2 Thessalonians 3:1-2 Should we also pray for other Christians and for the work of the Church? _____

No Barrier

"Perhaps it is sufficient to say that there are no barriers as to what you can bring to God in prayer. Our Heavenly Father is interested in everything we do, say, or think." (Bobby Bates)

Lesson 11
The Church:
Origin & Purpose

What is the Church?

The New Testament speaks of the Church frequently, with this word occurring over 100 times in Scripture. Apparently the Church is important, but what is the Church?

When you think of the "Church" what do you think about?
A building?
A denomination?
The collection of all denominations?

What does the word "Church" mean?

1. The Word "Church" in the original language literally means, "a *calling out*, that is, (concretely) a popular *meeting*, especially a religious *congregation*."[7]

---

[7] Strong's Hebrew and Greek Dictionaries.

2. Acts 8:1 Who or what was Saul persecuting? _____

3. Acts 9:1 Who or what was Saul persecuting?_____

  a. Was Saul persecuting the same thing/people in each instance?

_____

  b. Is "the Church" and "the disciples of the Lord" the same

thing? _____

  c. What is the Church? _____

4. 2 Thessalonians 2:14 How is the Church called? _____

_____

5. Acts 2:38, 47 Who is added to the "called out" (Church)? __

_____

6. 1 Peter 2:9 What are Christians "called out" of? _____

_____

7. Colossians 1:13 When one answers the call to come out of

darkness, Where does God place them? _____

In What ways does the New Testament use this word?

1. Matthew 16:18 Is Jesus talking about the entire Church here?

_____

2. Acts 20:28 Is the entire Church in view here? _____

3. 1 Corinthians 16:1 Is the entire Church being spoken of here?

_____

  a. To which Churches is Paul referring? _____

_____

4. 1 Corinthians 16:19 Is the entire Church being spoken of here?

_____

a. To which Churches is Paul referring? _____

_____

5. Ephesians 1:22-23, 4:4 How many Churches (bodies) are there?

_____

The word "Church" occurs in the plural form (Churches) 36 times in the New Testament. In each case it refers to congregations that are separated by distance, not doctrine. How else does the New Testament refer to the Church?

1. Colossians 1:18 What other name is used here to describe the Church? _____

2. Ephesians 5:22-25, Revelation 19:7-8 How is the Church portrayed here? _____

3. Ephesians 3:14-15 What term is used here to describe the Church? _____

4. 1 Timothy 3:15 What two terms are used here to describe the Church? _____

_____

5. Ephesians 2:19-22 How is the Church described here? _____

_____

a. **1 Corinthians 3:10-11** What foundation did the Apostles and prophets lay for the Church? _____

b. **Acts 4:10-12** What is the corner stone from which the entire Church is built and measured? _____

c. **1 Peter 2:5-8** What are the stones that make up the structure of the Church? _____

Used by Permission: WVBS

6. Matthew 16:18-19 What did Jesus promise to build? _____

_____

  a. To what did Jesus promise to give keys? _____

  b. Did Jesus use these two terms interchangeably here to speak

  of the same thing? _____

7. Acts 8:12 What was the subject of Philip's preaching? _____

_____

  a. Did their obedience to his preaching add them to the

  Kingdom? _____

  b. Did their obedience to his preaching add them to the

  Church? _____

8. Colossians 1:13 When were these Christians added to the Kingdom? _____

What is the Origin of the Church?

1. Matthew 16:15-19 Who built the Church? _____

   a. To whom does the Church belong? _____

   b. Will the Church ever be destroyed by Satan? _____

   c. What fact did Peter confess? _____

   d. From what source did Peter get this information? _____

   e. Is this fact the firm foundation stone upon which the Church is built? _____

When did God first envision the Church?

1. Ephesians 3:9-11 How long has the mystery of Christian fellowship been hidden in the mind of God? _____

_____

   a. How has God intended to reveal His manifold wisdom? __

_____

   b. How long has Christ and the Church been a part of God's plan and purpose? _____

2. Ephesians 1:3-4 Where has God placed all spiritual blessings?

_____

   a. Are there any spiritual blessings to be found outside of the Church (Christ)? _____

   b. When did God decide that those who are in the Church (Christ) should be saved? _____

When and where was the Church established?

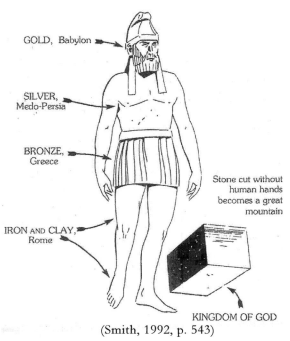

**REPRESENTS IN ITS TOTALITY
ALL HUMAN GOVERNMENT**

GOLD, Babylon ➤

SILVER,
Medo-Persia

BRONZE,
Greece

Stone cut without
human hands
becomes a great
mountain

IRON AND CLAY,
Rome

KINGDOM OF GOD

(Smith, 1992, p. 543)

1. Daniel 2:36-45 During which Kingdom was the Church
(Kingdom) to be established? _____

2. Joel 2:28-32 How did God say the Kingdom would be
established? _____

_____

3. Micah 4:1-2 Where did God say that the Law would go forth
from? _____

4. John 18:36-37 Was Jesus' Kingdom ever supposed to be
established on Earth? _____

5. Mark 9:1 When did Jesus say His Kingdom would come? __

_____

  a. How did Jesus say His Kingdom would come? _____

_____

6. Luke 24:49 Where would the apostles receive this power? __

_____

7. Acts 1:8 How would the apostles receive this power? _____

_____

8. Acts 2:1-4 When and where did the apostles receive this power?

_____

9. Acts 2:14-21 When did the "last days" begin? _____

_____

  a. Was this the proper time for the establishment of the
Kingdom according to prophecy? _____

  b. Was this the proper place for the establishment of the
Kingdom according to prophecy? _____

  c. Was this the proper method for the establishment of the
Kingdom according to prophecy? _____

Who established the Church?

1. Matthew 16:18 Who did Jesus say would build the Church?

_____

2. Acts 2:32-33 Who established the Church? _____

3. Acts 4:10-12 If a church was established by somebody other than Jesus can one be saved by becoming a part of that church?

_____

4. If a church was established in a place other than Jerusalem can one be saved by becoming a part of that church? _____

5. If a church was established at some time other than the first century AD can one be saved by becoming a part of that church?

_____

What is the Purpose of the Church?

1. 2 Timothy 1:9 Does God have a purpose for the Church (those that are in Christ)? _____

  a. How long has He had this purpose? _____

Is the Church important?

1. Acts 20:28 What was purchased by the blood of Christ? ____

_____

2. Ephesians 5:25 What did Jesus give His life for? _____

_____

3. Does Jesus think that the Church is important? _____

4. Should the Church be important to you? _____

What does the Church do?

1. Ephesians 3:10 How is God's Wisdom made known today?

_____

2. Romans 1:16-17 What reveals the righteousness and wisdom of God? _____

    a. Can God's wisdom be made known any other way? _____

3. Matthew 28:18-20 Who has the responsibility to make God's Wisdom known? _____

    a. Does that include you? _____

4. Romans 10:13-15 Will the Gospel be spread if the Church does not do it? _____

Fewer than three out of every 200 Americans are Christians.
(http://pewforum.org/)[8]

5. Ephesians 3:21 Where is God glorified? _____

_____

[8] Picture by timbuckteeth

a. Is it possible to glorify God anywhere else? _____

6. John 4:23-24 Does God expect the Church to glorify Him through proper worship?_____

7. Matthew 5:16 Does God expect the Church to glorify Him through the way that Christians live? _____

8. 1 Timothy 3:15 Does God expect the Church to glorify Him by upholding the truth? _____

    a. Does this include defending the truth against attacks? _____

    b. Does this include defending the truth against apathy? _____

    c. Does this include opposing error? _____

Works Cited

Smith, J. E. (1992). Old Testament Survey Series: The Major Prophets (Ppaerback ed.). Joplin, MO, United States of America: College Press Publishing Company.

Summary

The Church is:

> The saved
>
> Those called out of the world by the Gospel
>
> The Kingdom
>
> The Bride of Christ
>
> The Body of Christ
>
> The Household/Family of God

The word "Churches" appears in the New Testament only to refer to congregations in different locations.

The Church was in God's eternal plan even before He created the world.

The establishment of the Church was prophesied.

> It was established during the Roman Empire
>
> It was established during the life-time of those that heard Jesus
>
> It was established with power from the Holy Spirit
>
> It was established in Jerusalem

The Church was built by Jesus.

The Church has a very definite purpose in God's plan.

> Jesus died specifically for the Church
>
> It is to make His Wisdom known
>
>> By spreading the Gospel
>
> It is to glorify God
>
>> By worshipping Him
>>
>> By living as an example
>>
>> By upholding Truth
>>
>> By opposing error

Lesson 12
The Church, Her Design

Why are there so many Churches?

1. 1 Corinthians 1:10-13 Does loyalty to people instead of Christ and the Church cause division? _____

2. 1 Corinthians 11:18-22 Does a lack of brotherly love and compassion cause division? _____

3. 1 Timothy 6:3-5 Is division caused by a teaching that is different from the New Testament? _____

   a. Does pride cause division? _____

   b. Does a lack of knowledge cause division? _____

4. Matthew 15:3 Do traditions cause division? _____

5. Matthew 15:9 Do the doctrines of men cause division? _____

6. Matthew 15:13 If a Church is not like the Church of the New Testament can it be acceptable to God? _____

The Body of Christ – Modern View

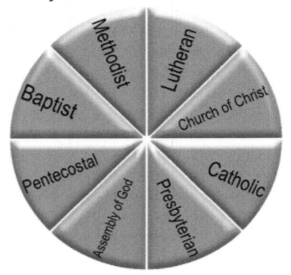

Used by Permission, Rick Brumback

7. Ephesians 4:4-5 How many Churches did God plant? _____

8. John 17:20-22 Did God intend for the Church to be united in its teaching, worship, and practice? _____

  a. If two Churches are different can they both be the Church of the Bible? _____

  b. If two Churches are different can they both *not* be the Church of the Bible? _____

The Body of Christ – God's View

John 17:20-22

1 Corinthians 1:10

One Origin
One Teaching
One Practice

Used by Permission, Rick Brumback

What makes Christ's Church unique?

Her Creed

1. 2 John 9-11 Can anybody follow a teaching that is different from the New Testament and become a part of Christ's Church?

_____

2. Revelation 22:18-19 Can anybody make additions, subtractions, or substitutions to the New Testament and be in unity with Christ's Church? _____

3. Does the Church that you are a part of practice or teach anything that is not in the New Testament, or do they fail to practice or teach anything that *is* in the New Testament? _____

Does Not Have God

Does Not Have Christ

2 John 9-11

Revelation 22:18-19

Doctrine of Christ

Her Terms of Admission

1. Mark 16:15-16 Can anybody fail to believe the Gospel and become a part of Christ's Church? _____

2. Luke 13:3 Can anybody fail to repent and become a part of Christ's Church? _____

3. Matthew 10:32-33 Can anybody fail to confess Christ and become a part of Christ's Church? _____

4. 1 Corinthians 12:13 Can anybody fail to be baptized according to the teaching of Scripture and become a part of Christ's Church? _____

Her Mission

1. Matthew 28:18-20 Is the New Testament Church focused on teaching the Gospel to the Lost and saving souls? _____

2. Ephesians 4:11-16 Is the New Testament Church focused on educating her members and strengthening their faith? _____

    a. Are the members of the New Testament Church dedicated to this same mission? _____

3. 2 Timothy 2:2 Should Christians share their faith and knowledge of Scripture with others so that they can grow and be able to do the same thing for others? _____

4. Galatians 6:10 Is the New Testament Church going to be concerned with giving benevolent aid to those who have a need?

_____

Her Worship

1. John 4:23-24 Is the New Testament Church going to worship in spirit *and* in Truth (according to New Testament teaching)?

_____

    a. Can a Church worship in a different way and still be Christ's Church? _____

2. The New Testament pattern for worship was covered in detail in lesson nine.

Her Organization

1. Ephesians 5:23 Who is the head of the Church? _____

2. Titus 1:5-7 If a Church does not have elders is it lacking something? _____

3. Hebrews 13:17 Are members of the Church to submit to the authority of the elders so long as they do not contradict the teaching of the Bible? _____

4. 1 Timothy 3:8-11 Does the Church of the New Testament also have deacons? _____

    a. Are the deacons, as well as the elders, to meet certain qualifications? _____

    b. Can a Church be Christ's Church without following this pattern as best as it can? _____

5. Philippians 1:1 Other than the Christians (saints), elders, and deacons, does the Bible speak of the Church having any other organization on earth? _____

Her Name

1. Ephesians 3:14-15 Who has the right to name the Church?

_____

   a. Can we give the Church a name that God has not given and be pleasing to Him? _____

2. Romans 16:16 Is Church of Christ an acceptable name? ____

3. Matthew 23:8 What family relationship do members of the Church have to one another in God's Family? _____

4. John 8:31 Can members of the Church be called disciples? _

_____

5. Acts 11:26 Can members of the Church be called Christians?

_____

6. 1 Corinthians 1:2 Can members of the Church be called saints?

_____

Can the New Testament Church exist today?

1. Luke 8:11 What is the seed that produces Christians? _____

_____

2. Matthew 13:31-32 If a mustard seed is planted what will grow?

_____

   a. If the Word of God is planted will Christians grow? _____

   b. If the Word of God is planted will a Church grow? _____

   c. Will those Christians and that Church be Christ's Church that is found in the New Testament? _____

Summary

Division and multiple Churches are the result of sin and error.
Christ's Church is unique and has certain characteristics:

The Bible is Her only creed.

Her terms of admission are Bible based.

Her mission: Evangelism, edification, benevolence

Her worship: in spirit and Truth

Her organization: Christ, elders, deacons, & saints

Her name is God-given

The New Testament Church can exist today

The seed is the Word of God

The Bible only makes Christians only and only
Christians.

Lesson 13
The Church, My Relationship & Responsibilities

What is my relationship to the Church?

1. Acts 2:47 Who does God add to the Church? _____

_____

    a. When does God add them to the Church? _____

    _____

2. Galatians 3:26-29 How does one get into Christ (the Church)?

    _____

    a. Should all Christians view all other Christians as equals and

    peers within the Church? _____

3. 1 Corinthians 12:4-11 Do Christians have different abilities and

    different levels of abilities? _____

a. Who gives us the abilities that we have (**v. 6**)? _____

b. Are these abilities designed to be used for the benefit of all? (**v. 7**) _____

c. Does God expect Christians to use their abilities to work together for the common purpose of glorifying Him? (**v. 11**)

_____

4. **1 Corinthians 12:12-21** What is the basis for our unity as Christians (**v. 12-13**)? _____

a. Is it a part of God's plan and design for the Church that it be made up of people who are different? (**v. 14-18**)? _____

b. Could the Church be complete if we discriminated against others who were different from ourselves (**v. 19-21**)?

_____

5. **1 Corinthians 12:22-26** Are the Christians who are weakest in their faith or ability necessary for the Church (**v. 22**)? _____

a. Should we, as Christians, care for one another spiritually and help to fill each other's weaknesses (**v. 23-25**)? _____

b. Should we care emotionally for one another as Christians (**v. 26**)? _____

6. **1 Corinthians 12:27-31** Is it okay that one Christian may not have the abilities that another Christian has (**V. 27-30**)? _____

a. Should we strive to grow and increase our abilities (**v. 31**)?

_____

Justin Hopkins

What are my responsibilities to the Church?

1. 1 Timothy 3:15 Does God expect us to live and act in a certain way as Christians? _____

   a. Is a Christian, as a part of the Body, always "in the Church?"

   _____

   b. Do a Christian's actions affect the Church of which he/she is a member? _____

2. Hebrews 10:23-26 Is it important for a Christian to actively maintain his/her faith and convictions in Christ? _____

   a. Do we have an obligation to watch for the souls of the Christians around us and to encourage them in the Faith (**v. 24**)? _____

   b. Can we fulfill that obligation if we are willfully absent from the meetings of the Church (**v. 25**)? _____

   c. Is it a sin to be willfully absent from the meetings of the Lord's Church (**v. 26**)? _____

3. Galatians 6:1-2 If you see another Christian fall into a sin, either by doing something that is wrong, or by failing to obey a command do you have an obligation to try to restore that brother? _____

   a. How are we to do this? _____

   b. Should we always maintain an awareness of our own ability to sin? _____

c. Can we fulfill Christ's Law if we fail to care spiritually for one another? _____

4. James 5:16 Can your brethren effectively care for your soul if they do not know your struggles? _____

5. Matthew 5:23-24 Can a Christian offer acceptable worship to God if he/she is at strife with another? _____

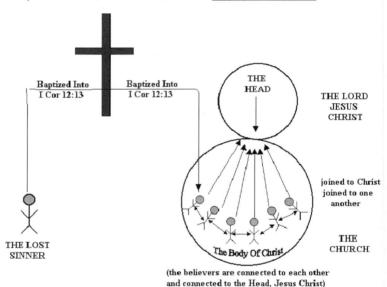

(the believers are connected to each other and connected to the Head, Jesus Christ)

6. Matthew 18:15-17 If you see another Christian in sin, should you first tell others about it, or go talk to them in private? _

_____

a. If your brother does not repent after you have gone to them in private do you still have an obligation to them? _____

b. What is the next thing you should do, and why? _____

_____

c. If they still will not repent, what is your final obligation?

_____

d. If they still refuse to repent, can you maintain your relationship with that wayward Christian as before? _____

What is the Church's responsibility to me?

1. **Do other Christians have the same responsibilities to me that I have toward them?** _____

2. 1 Peter 5:1-5 Do the elders have the responsibility to make a healthy diet of spiritual nutrition available to me? _____

a. Do elders have the responsibility to keep an eye on (oversee) my spiritual health? _____

b. Should elders be motivated by obligation, money, or a desire to serve? _____

c. Should elders lead by tyranny or by example? _____

3. 1 Corinthians 5:1-11 If I fall into sin can the Christians around me ignore my sin and act as though everything is okay?**(v. 1-2)**

_____

a. If I refuse to repent of my sin, what is the Church's obligation to me? **(v. 3-5)** _____

b. What is the first purpose that is given for withdrawal of fellowship **(v. 5b)**? _____

c. What is the second purpose that is given for withdrawal of fellowship **(v. 6)**? _____

d. Can the Church be kept pure and acceptable to God if we fail to withdraw from wayward Christians? (**v. 7-8**) _____

e. Can a faithful Christian maintain a casual relationship with a wayward unrepentant Christian? (**v. 9-11**) _____

f. Why/why not? _____

_____

g. Can a faithful Christian maintain a casual relationship with non-Christians and hope to bring them to Christ? (**v. 10**)?

_____

h. Why/why not? _____

_____

i. Will withdrawal of fellowship be effective if some Christians do not follow through with what this passage teaches?

_____

4. 2 Thessalonians 3:6-15 If I am not living according to the commands (traditions) given in the New Testament, what is the Church's responsibility to me? (**v. 6**) _____

a. Is this responsibility laid on the Church as a "formal proceeding" or on the individual Christian as an action? __

_____

b. What is the purpose given here for withdrawing from a wayward Christian? (**v. 14**) _____

c. How should the one that is withdrawn from be treated"? (**v. 15**) _____

_____

d. When you see a Christian who has been withdrawn from what are you to do (**v. 15b**)? _____

5. 2 Corinthians 2:6-11 Was the withdrawal of fellowship effective in restoring this brother (**v. 6**)? _____

a. When a Christian is restored how are other Christians to respond? (**v. 7-8**) _____

_____

b. What might happen in that Christian's life if they are not received with love (**v. 7**)? _____

c. What is the danger to the Church as a whole if God's plan for discipline is not followed (**v. 11**)? _____

_____

Summary

As a Christian I am a part of the Church.

> I was added to the Church by God.
>
> This happened when I was baptized into Christ.
>
> Christians have different abilities.
>
> We work together for the glory of God.

As a Christian I have a responsibility to the Church.

> The Church is affected by my conduct.
>
> I have a responsibility to attend services.
>
> I have a responsibility to encourage my brethren.
>
> I have a responsibility to restore the fallen.

The Church (other Christians) has a responsibility to me.

> The Church watches for my soul.
>
> The Church provides spiritual nourishment.
>
> The Church tries to restore me when I fall into sin.
>
> God has a plan that is effective to fulfill this role.

Lesson 14
Who Art Thou Lord?

Is it important to understand who God is?

1. John 17:3 What is required for eternal life? _____

_____

2. 2 Thessalonians 1:7-9 What will happen to those who do not

know God? _____

3. Genesis 1:26 If you are made in the image of God can you

properly understand yourself without understanding God? ____

_____

4. Acts 17:22-23 Did the Athenians understand who God is? _

_____

   a. Were they worshipping God? _____

   b. Was their worship acceptable to God? _____

   c. Can we properly worship God as we should if we do not

understand who He is? _____

What is God like?

1. John 4:24 What is God? _____

2. Luke 24:39 Does a spirit have a physical body? _____

Eternal

3. Isaiah 48:12 Did anything or anyone exist before God? ____

    a. Will anything or anyone exist after God? _____

4. Psalm 90:2 How long has God existed? _____

    a. How long will God continue to exist? _____

5. Exodus 3:14 Does God depend on anybody or anything outside of Himself for His existence? _____

    a. Does that imply God's eternal nature? _____

Immutable

1. Malachi 3:6 Does God ever change? _____

2. James 1:17 Is there even a hint (shadow) that God might change? _____

Omnipresent

1. Jeremiah 23:23-24 Is there any place that one can go where God is not present? _____

    a. Does God exist in every place at every moment? _____

2. Proverbs 15:3 Where does God see us? _____

    a. Is this true all the time? _____

    b. Does God see all that we do? _____

Omnipotent

1. Job 42:1-2 How many things is God able to do? _____

    a. Is anything beyond the power of God? _____

2. Matthew 19:26 How many things are possible with God? __

_____

3. Revelation 19:6 Is God all-powerful? _____

    a. Is there anything that God cannot do? _____

    b. Can God limit Himself if He so desires? _____

4. Titus 1:2, James 1:13 Can God do something that contradicts His nature? _____

    a. Is this one way that God limits Himself? _____

    b. Does this mean that God is not omnipotent? _____

Omniscient

1. 1 John 3:20 How many things does God know? _____

    a. Is there anything that God does not know? _____

2. Psalm 147:5 How large is God's capacity for knowledge and understanding? _____

3. Acts 15:8 Does God know everything that we think or feel?

_____

Who is Jesus?

1. John 1:1-5 When was the Word with God? _____

    a. What/who is the Word? _____

    b. Who made all things? _____

    c. Is the Word life? _____

    d. Is the Word light? _____

2. John 1:14 What form did the Word assume? _____

    a. Did people see His glory? _____

    b. How is that glory described? _____

    _____

    c. Is the Word Jesus Christ? _____

3. Hebrews 3:4 Who created all things? _____

    a. Did Jesus create all things (John 1:3)? _____

    b. Is Jesus God? _____

4. Philippians 2:5-11 Was Jesus equal with God before He came
to earth? _____

    a. What did Jesus do when He came to Earth? _____

    _____

Eternal

1. John 8:57-59 Is Jesus statement here basically the same as what
God said in Exodus 3:14? _____

    a. Does that imply that Jesus is eternal? _____

    b. Does that imply that Jesus is God? _____

2. Hebrews 1:8-9; Psalm 45:6-7 Are these two passages the same?

_____

    a. Is Jesus God? _____

    b. For how long is Jesus' throne? _____

3. Hebrews 1:10-12; Psalm 102:25-27 Who is the Hebrew writer
talking about here? _____

    a. Does Jesus change? _____

b. Is Jesus eternal? _____

c. IN PSALM 102:22 JEHOVAH (LORD) is used.

d. Is Jesus Jehovah? _____

Immutable

1. Hebrews 13:8 Has Jesus ever changed? _____

    a. Will Jesus ever change? _____

Omnipresent

1. Matthew 28:20 Is Jesus going to be with Christians until the end of the world? _____

    a. With how many Christians will He be present? _____

    b. Does this require Jesus to occupy an unknown number of locations at all times? _____

2. Colossians 1:17 Do all things exist by (literally in) Christ? __

_____

    a. If all that exists is in Christ is there any place where Christ is not present? _____

Omnipotent

1. Philippians 4:13 How many things can we do through Christ?

_____

    a. Could Christ enable us to do something that He cannot do?

_____

2. Hebrews 1:3 Who sustains all things by His word of power?

_____

Omniscient

1. John 21:17 How many things does Jesus know? _____

    a. Is there anything that Jesus does not know? _____

2. John 2:24 How much does Jesus know about us? _____

3. Hebrews 4:12-13 All things are naked and open before the eyes of whom? _____

    a. Who is the Word? _____

    b. Is Jesus omniscient? _____

Who is the Holy Spirit?

1. 1 Timothy 4:1 What is the Holy Spirit *doing* in this verse? ___

_____

    a. Can a "force" that is not a person do this? _____

2. 1 Corinthians 12:11 Does the Holy Spirit have a will, or desire?

_____

    a. Can a "force" that is not a person have a will? _____

3. Ephesians 4:30 Can the Holy Spirit be grieved? _____

    a. Can a "force" that is not a person be grieved? _____

4. Acts 16:6-7 What did the Holy Spirit do here? _____

_____

    a. Can a "force" that is not a person forbid? _____

    b. Is the Holy Spirit a person? _____

5. Acts 5:3 To whom did Satan tempt Ananias to lie? _____

_____

    a. Did he lie to the Holy Spirit? _____

6. Acts 5:4 To whom did Peter say he had lied? _____

_____

    a. Did he lie to God? _____

    b. Is the Holy Spirit God? _____

7. Acts 7:51-52 Who did the ancient Jews resist? _____

    a. How did they do this? _____

_____

8. Nehemiah 9:26, 32 Is Nehemiah speaking of the same people

and events as Steven (Acts 7)? _____

    a. Against whom did Steven say these people rebelled? ____

_____

    b. Did Nehemiah say that this was God? _____

    c. Is the Holy Spirit God? _____

9. Luke 4:18-19 Who anointed Jesus to preach the Gospel? __

_____

10. Isaiah 61:1-2 Who anointed Jesus to preach the Gospel? __

_____

    a. Is the Holy Spirit Jehovah? _____

11. John 14:26 Who would God send to the apostles? _____

_____

    a. Does this imply that the Holy Spirit has a relationship to

God the Father as a distinct individual? _____

12. John 16:12-14 Did the Holy Spirit guide the apostles? _____

    a. Did the Holy Spirit speak to the apostles? _____

    b. Does the Holy Spirit hear? _____

c. Did the Holy Spirit receive something? _____

d. From whom did the Holy Spirit receive His message? __

_____

e. Does this imply that the Holy Spirit has a relationship with God the Son as a distinct individual? _____

Eternal

1. Hebrews 9:14 Is the Holy Spirit eternal? _____

    a. Does the Holy Spirit have a beginning? _____

    b. Will the Holy Spirit have an end? _____

Omnipresent

1. Psalm 139:7-10 Is there anywhere that one could go that the Holy Spirit is not there? _____

2. 1 Corinthians 3:16 Does the Holy Spirit dwell in every Christian simultaneously? _____

    a. Would this require the Holy Spirit to occupy an unknown number of locations at every moment? _____

Omnipotent

1. Job 26:13 Did the Holy Spirit create the hosts of the heavens?

_____

2. Job 33:4 Who created man? _____

3. Romans 8:11 Did the Holy Spirit raise Christ from the dead?

_____

Omniscient

1. Isaiah 40:13-14 Has there ever been another being that was capable of teaching the Holy Spirit something that He does not know? _____

2. 1 Corinthians 2:9-11 Is God the Father omniscient? _____

    a. Does the Holy Spirit know everything that God knows?

_____

    b. Is there anything that the Holy Spirit does not know? __

_____

How many Gods are there?

1. Deuteronomy 6:4-5 How many Gods are there? _____

2. Isaiah 44:6-8 Is there more than one God revealed in the Bible?

_____

3. Matthew 4:10 How many beings are we to worship? _____

4. Acts 10:25-26 Is it a sin to offer worship to a human being?

_____

5. Revelation 22:8-9 Is it a sin to offer worship to an angel?

_____

    a. Who is the only one that can receive worship? _____

The Unity of God

1. Isaiah 46:9 How many gods are there? _____

    a. Did the Son and the Holy Spirit exist when this was said?

_____

2. 1 Kings 8:60 Is there any God other than Jehovah (the LORD)?

_____

    a. Is God the Father called Jehovah? _____

    b. Is God the Son called Jehovah? _____

    c. Is God the Holy Spirit called Jehovah? _____

3. Galatians 3:20 How is God described? _____

4. John 17:21 Are Christ and the Father one? _____

The Distinctions of God

1. 2 Corinthians 13:14 Are these three presented as being distinct one from another? _____

2. Matthew 3:16-17 Are all three persons of the godhead shown in this event? _____

    a. How is the Father seen? _____

    b. How is the Son seen? _____

    c. How is the Spirit seen? _____

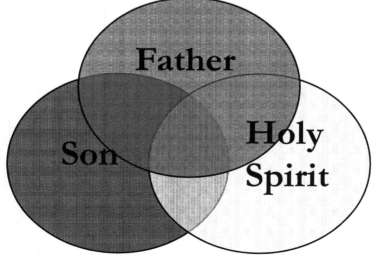

3. John 4:23-24 Are we obligated to worship the Father? _____

4. John 9:35-38 Did Jesus accept worship from humans while on earth? _____

    a. Is it still proper for humans to worship him now that He is in Heaven? _____

5. Hebrews 1:6 Do the angels have an obligation to worship Jesus?

_____

    a. If the angels have such an obligation, do we also have this obligation? _____

6. Ephesians 2:18 Is the Holy Spirit essential in our worship to God? _____

Summary

It is important to understand who God is.
> This is required for eternal life.
> Those who do not know God will be destroyed.
> One cannot know himself without knowing God.
> Not knowing God results in ignorant worship.

God is a spirit with no physical body.

God is Eternal.

God is immutable.

God is omnipresent.

God is omnipotent.
> There is nothing that God cannot do.
> God has the ability to limit Himself.
> God will not do that which is contrary to His nature.

God is omniscient.

Jesus is the second person of the Godhead
> He created all things.

He was fully equal with God.

He assumed human form and made Himself subject
 to God the Father for our sake.

Jesus is eternal.

 He is self-existent.

 He is Jehovah.

Jesus is immutable.

Jesus is Omnipresent.

Jesus is Omnipotent.

Jesus is Omniscient.

The Holy Spirit is the third person of the Godhead.

He is a person, not an impersonal force.

He has a will.

He can be grieved.

He can forbid and teach.

The Holy Spirit is Jehovah.

The Holy Spirit is Eternal.

The Holy Spirit is Omnipresent.

The Holy Spirit is Omnipotent.

The Holy Spirit is Omniscient.

God is one, composed of three distinct personalities.

Lesson 15
What About Miracles?

What is the Purpose of a Miracle?

To Show that Jesus is God

1. Mark 2:5-12 Does anybody other than God have the authority to forgive sins? _____

    a. How did Jesus prove that He has the authority to forgive sins? _____

2. John 10:24-25 What evidence did Jesus provide which proved that He is the Messiah? _____

3. John 10:37-38 Should we believe Jesus if He did not work any miracles? _____

    a. Did Jesus work miracles? _____

    b. Should we believe His claims to be the Messiah? _____

4. Acts 2:22 How did God show that Jesus' claims were true? _

_____

5. John 20:30-31 Were all of Jesus' miracles written down for us today? _____

    a. Why were some of His miracles recorded? _____

    _____

    b. Are the recorded miracles sufficient evidence to produce faith? _____

To Reveal the Word

1. John 14:26 How many things would the Holy Spirit miraculously teach to the Apostles? _____

2. John 16:12-13 How much truth would the Holy Spirit miraculously reveal to the Apostles? _____

3. 1 John 1:3-4 What did the Apostles do with their knowledge of the Gospel? _____

4. 2 Peter 1:20-21 Did the written Word come from man? ____

    a. How did the writers of the Bible know what to say? _____

    _____

To Confirm the Word

1. Mark 16:17-20 Did God give the ability to perform miracles to some Christians during the first century? _____

    a. What did these Christians do every time a miracle was performed? _____

    b. What was the purpose of the miracles? _____

    _____

2. Hebrews 2:3-4 Who began to speak of our salvation? _____

_____

   a. Who continued the work of declaring our salvation? __

_____

   b. How was the truth of their words confirmed? _____

_____

Preaching   **Performing Miracles**   **Word is believed**

Does God still allow Miracles Today?

1. 1 Corinthians 13:8-10 Did the miraculous gifts of prophecy and speaking in other languages (tongues) give a complete knowledge of the Gospel? _____

   a. Were these miraculous gifts "in part"? _____

   b. When would these miraculous gifts cease? _____

_____

2. James 1:21-25 What is able to save your soul (**v. 21**)? _____

_____

147

a. Is the Word perfect (**v.25**)? _____

3. Jude 3 Has the Word of God been completely revealed? ____

a. When Did Jude say that the Word of God had been

completely revealed? _____

b. If the Word of God has been once and for all time delivered,

will God reveal any additional information to anybody in any

way? _____

c. Has "that which is perfect" come? _____

4. 2 Peter 1:3 Has God given us everything that we need to know

for life and godliness? _____

a. Do we need anything other than the Gospel in order to be

able to be pleasing to God? _____

5. 2 Timothy 3:16-17 How were the Scriptures given to us? __

_____

a. Does the Word of God give us everything that we need to

be pleasing to God? _____

b. Is it possible to do a good work that requires more than

just the Word of God to be able to do this good work?

_____

How was miraculous power given?

1. Acts 1:5-8 Who was given this promise of receiving miraculous

power? (**v. 2**) _____

a. When would they receive this power? _____

_____

b. Where would they receive this power? _____

2. Acts 1:26-2:4 When did this happen? _____

_____

    a. Was this a fulfillment of the promise found in chapter one?_____

    b. Who received this miraculous power (**v. 26**)? _____

_____

3. Acts 8:5-8 Did Philip work miracles when he preached? ____

    a. What effect did these miracles have on those that heard him?

_____

_____

4. Acts 8:13-19 Was Simon baptized into Christ for salvation? _

_____

    a. Did he spend time with Philip after his conversion? (**v. 13**)

_____

_____

    b. Had any of the new Christians received the ability to work miracles? (**v. 16**) _____

    c. Did Simon ask Philip to give him this ability? _____

    d. Why did Peter and John come all the way from Jerusalem? (**v. 14-15**) _____

    e. How was the ability to work miracles given? (**v. 18**) _____

_____

    f. Since he was not an apostle could Philip have given others the ability to work miracles? _____

What does that mean for us today?

1. Are any of the apostles alive today? _____

2. Is anybody who has ever seen one of the apostles alive today?

_____

_____

3. Is it possible for anybody to receive the ability to work miracles

today? _____

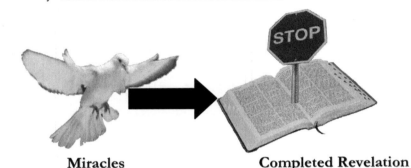

Miracles   **Completed Revelation**

What about people who claim to work miracles?

1. 1 Corinthians 14:37 Should we believe anybody who claims to

teach the truth who does not agree with what has been revealed in

Scripture? _____

2. 1 John 4:1 Should we believe everybody who claims to be a

teacher of truth? _____

    a. Why/why not? _____

_____

3. 1 John 4:6 How can we know the difference between those that teach truth and those that teach error? _____

_____

4. 2 Thessalonians 2:9-12 Will some teachers of satanic doctrine appear to work miracles and signs? _____

    a. Will they deceive a number of people? _____

    b. Will God allow those who are not careful to believe the lies of these teachers? _____

    c. Why? _____

5. 2 Corinthians 11:13-15 Will false teachers claim to be servants of Christ? _____

    a. Why should we not be surprised by this? _____

_____

6. 2 Peter 2:1-2 What will happen to these false teachers? _____

_____

    a. What will happen to those who are deceived by these false teachers? _____

7. Acts 17:11 What should we do to avoid being deceived? ____

_____

Summary

Miracles were performed in the first century for special purposes:

> To show that Jesus is God.
>
> To reveal the Gospel to man.
>
> To confirm the Word that was revealed.

Miracles were allowed for a limited time only.

> They would cease after the Gospel was completely revealed.
>
> The Gospel has been completely revealed.

The ability to work miracles was given only by the laying on of the apostles' hands.

> There are no apostles alive today.
>
> Therefore there can be no miracles today.

All who serve Christ must acknowledge the truth of His Word.

> His Word says that miracles have ceased.
>
> Those who claim to work miracles are false teachers.
>
> Those who are deceived by false teachers will be condemned.
>
> We must compare everything that we are taught to what the Bible says so that we are not deceived.

Lesson 16
The End of All Things

What happens when we die?

1. Hebrews 9:27 How many times will you die? _____

    a. What will happen to you after you die? _____

    b. Is it possible to die, come back to life, and then die again?

    _____

    c. Is it possible to be re-incarnated (brought back to life in a

    different form) after you die? _____

2. Ecclesiastes 12:7 What will happen to your physical body when

you die? _____

    a. What will happen to your soul/spirit when you die? _____

    _____

    b. Will your soul remain with your body in the grave? _____

3. Matthew 10:28 When you die is your soul destroyed? _____

    a. How can your soul be destroyed? _____

4. Luke 16:19-23 Did Jesus tell this story as a parable (the Kingdom of Heaven is like . . .), or as something that actually happened? _____

   a. Where did Lazarus find himself after he died? _____

   _____

   b. How long after he died did this happen? _____

   c. Where did the rich man find himself after he died? _____

   _____

   d. How long after he died did this happen? _____

5. Luke 16:23-26 Could the rich man see Lazarus in paradise?

_____

   a. Does Jesus say that Lazarus could see the rich man in torment? _____

   b. What is between Paradise and Torment? _____

   _____

   c. Is it possible for anybody to go from Paradise to Torment?

   _____

   d. Is it possible for anybody to go from Torment to Paradise?

   _____

6. Luke 16:27-31 Does God allow anybody to come back from the dead or to communicate with the living after they have died?

_____

   a. If somebody did come back from the dead would that be more effective than the Gospel to cause someone to repent?

   _____

b. What is the most effective, and only way that God persuades us to obey Him? _____

7. Luke 23:42-43 Where did Jesus and the thief go after they died?

_____

    a. How long after their deaths did they get there? _____

_____

What happens when Christ returns?

1. 1 Corinthians 15:24-26 When will Jesus stop reigning over the Church (His Kingdom)? _____

    a. How long *must* He reign? _____

_____

    b. What is the last enemy that He will conquer? _____

2. 1 Corinthians 15:35-38 When a seed is planted does the seed have to be destroyed before a plant will grow in its place?

_____

    a. When you die will the body that is resurrected be the same as the one you have now? _____

3. 1 Corinthians 15:44, 50 What kind of a body will you have at the resurrection? _____

    a. Is it possible for your physical body to enter Heaven? __

4. 1 Corinthians 15:51-54 Will everybody die before Jesus returns? **(v. 51)** _____

    a. Will everybody's body be transformed into a spiritual body when Jesus returns? **(v. 51)** _____

b. How quickly will the resurrection and transformation take place? (**v. 52**) _____

5. 1 Thessalonians 4:13-18 When Jesus returns how will His arrival be announced? (**v. 16**) _____

_____

　　a. Will those who have already died be raised before or after those who are alive? (**v. 16**) _____

　　b. What will happen to those who are still alive? (**v. 17**) ____

_____

　　c. Will Jesus ever set foot on the earth? _____

6. John 5:28-29 How many of those who are dead will be resurrected? _____

　　a. Will all who have done good be resurrected? _____

　　b. What will happen to them at the resurrection? _____

_____

　　c. Will all who have done evil be resurrected? _____

　　d. What will happen to them at the resurrection? _____

_____

7. 1 Thessalonians 5:1-6 Will there be any signs to tell us that Jesus is about to return? _____

　　a. Will the world be expecting Jesus' return when it happens?

_____

　　b. Will there be any time to repent or to escape when Jesus returns? _____

c. Should we as Christians be caught off guard by Jesus' return?

_____

8. 2 Peter 3:9-15 Why is it taking so long for Jesus to return in judgment? (**v. 9**) _____

_____

    a. What will happen to the earth and to the entire universe when Jesus returns? (**v. 10**) _____

_____

    b. If even the elements will melt, will there be anything left of the earth after it is destroyed?(**v. 12**) _____

    c. What should we do to prepare for Christ's return? (**v. 14-15**)

_____

What happens after that?

1. 2 Corinthians 5:10 Who will be our judge? _____

    a. How many people will be judged by Jesus? _____

    b. What will our judgment be based on? _____

2. John 12:48 What is the standard that Jesus will use to judge us?

_____

3. Matthew 25:31-34 When Jesus returns where will He sit? __

_____

    a. How many people will Jesus judge? _____

    b. What will He tell to those who have obeyed Him? _____

_____

4. Matthew 25:41, 46 What will Jesus tell to those who have not obeyed Him? _____

    a. How long will the reward for obedience last? _____

    _____

    b. How long will the punishment for disobedience last? ____

    _____

5. Mark 9:45-48 Will those who have disobeyed Christ ever die or stop being punished? _____

6. Revelation 14:11-13 How long will those that are lost be tormented? _____

    a. Will they ever get a break from their torment? _____

    b. What will happen to those who are faithful to God? ____

    _____

7. Matthew 6:19-21 Where will we receive our reward if we live faithful to Christ? _____

8. 2 Corinthians 5:1 Where will be the eternal dwelling place of those that are found faithful? _____

    a. Will anybody receive their reward somewhere else? _____

    _____

9. 1 Peter 1:3-4 Where is our inheritance? _____

    a. Will our inheritance ever be spent or lose its value? _____

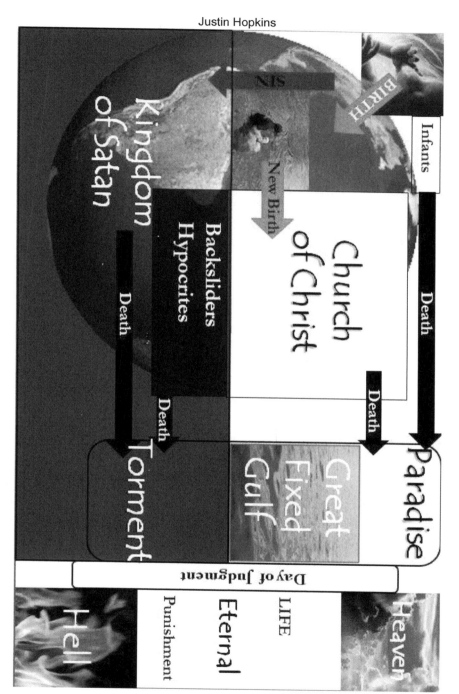

Summary

When we die we go immediately to either Paradise or Torment.

> There is no way to pass from Torment to Paradise, or vice versa.
>
> We get no second chance at life, and are judged by the way we live this life.

When Christ returns all the dead will be raised.

> Those that are still alive will also meet Him in the air.
>
> There will be no signs or warning.
>
> Our bodies will be transformed to be spiritual bodies.
>
> We will all be judged by the Gospel.

After judgment everybody will go either to Heaven or Hell.

> Hell is a place of eternal punishment.
>
> This punishment will last forever with no rest.
>
> Heaven is a place of eternal reward.
>
> We will be with Jesus.
>
> We will rest and be comforted.
>
> We will be in Heaven with Christ forever.

Lesson 17
Sharing The Good News

The Great Commission

1. Luke 19:10 What was Jesus' sole purpose for coming to Earth?

_____

    a. Should our main goal in life be the same as His? _____

    b. If our main goal in life is different from His, can we truly be

    His followers? _____

2. Luke 24:46-47 Is the sharing of the Gospel a part of God's

eternal plan? _____

3. Romans 10:13-15 Is it possible for a person to be saved if they

do not hear the Gospel? _____

4. Ephesians 3:10-11 How does God plan to make the Gospel

known? _____

    a. How long has this been God's plan? _____

5. Matthew 28:18-20 To whom is Jesus speaking? _____

a. What is the first thing that He commanded them to do (**v. 19a**)? _____

b. What is the second thing that He commanded them to do (**v. 19b**)? _____

c. What is the third thing that He commanded them to do (**v. 20**)? _____

d. Does this include us? _____

e. Does "all things whatsoever I have commanded you" include the three commands given here? _____

6. Ezekiel 3:18 Will God hold us accountable if we fail to share the Gospel with those that need to hear it? _____

7. John 15:2 What does it mean to bear fruit? _____

_____

a. What will happen to those Christians who do not bear fruit?

_____

8. James 5:20 What is the result of sharing the Gospel to a person if they are obedient? _____

Overcoming Ourselves

1. "I don't have time."

a. Do you have time to watch TV, use the internet, etc? ___

b. Matthew 6:33 Do you have time to eat? _____

c. If the Church is your top priority will you have time to share the Gospel? _____

2. "I'm supporting the work."

a. Is the command to give of your means for every Christian?

_____

b. Is the command to teach all nations for every Christian?

_____

c. Can someone else give for you? _____

d. Can someone else evangelize for you? _____

3. "I am teaching by example."

a. According to **Romans 10:14-15** can others hear the Gospel if it is not preached? _____

b. Is living a good example enough to fulfill the Great Commission? _____

4. "I don't know enough to teach others."

a. **Luke 24:47** What two things must be taught in order to share the Gospel? _____

b. Have you obeyed the Gospel yourself? _____

c. Can you show others from Scripture how and why to do what you did in order to receive salvation? _____

5. "I'm afraid of what others will think of me."

a. **Luke 9:26** What will Jesus do if we are too ashamed to share the Gospel? _____

b. Is it more important to be well thought of by your friends or by Jesus? _____

6. "People just aren't interested in the Gospel anymore."

a. **Matthew 13:3-9** Upon how many of these four soils did the sower sow the Word? _____

b. Upon how many of these four soils did the seed grow? _

_____

c. Should we also so the Word on every heart that we can?

_____

d. 1 Corinthians 3:6-7 Who gives the increase? _____

e. If a soul does not respond to the Word that we have planted or watered should we grow discouraged? _____

Who?

1. Mark 16:15-16 With whom did Jesus say we should share the Gospel? _____

2. John 4:34-35 Is there an abundance of souls who are ready to receive the Gospel? _____

FACT:

Dr. Winfield Arn of the Institute for American Church Growth has interviewed some 4,000 converts primarily on the American West Coast. **70-80% of these were invited by friends or relatives!**

Every Christian ought to strive to have at least three prospects at all times which they are praying for daily and actively seeking to bring to Christ.

Prospects are all around!

Family members & relatives

Friends

Co-workers

Schoolmates

Acquaintances

Online Friends

Neighbors

Business Contacts

Wait staff

Mechanics, etc.

Insurance Agents

Visitors at worship

Wayward Christians

_____

Relatives of Members

_____

Friends of Members

_____

Experiencing life changes

_____

Newcomer to community

_____

Experiencing hardship

_____

Experiencing illness

_____

"Loner"

_____

Prisoners

_____

Death in Family

_____

Asking Questions

_____

Religious

_____

Dissatisfied with denomination

_____

Others

_____

How?

Many possible methods of Evangelism:
1. Invite others to a Gospel Meeting/Worship service.
2. Pass out Gospel tracts.
   a. If your congregation has not made Gospel tracts available to you, then ask!
3. Pass out Searching for Truth DVD's.
4. Hold screenings of Searching for Truth.
5. Go Door knocking.
6. Use the written word.
   a. Church Bulletins
   b. Church Business cards
   c. Books
   d. Your own notes
   e. Recorded sermons
7. Send out correspondence courses.
8. Set up a fair booth.
9. Hold group Bible studies.
10. Hold one on one Bible studies.
    a. This is the best method.
    b. Start by being a silent partner.
11. Other Methods _____

_____

FOLLW UP, FOLLOW UP, FOLLOW UP!

How do I begin?

1. Matthew 5:14-16 What/who is the light if the world? _____

_____

    a. How would you hide your light "under a bushel?" _____

    _____

    b. How would you let your light shine? _____

    _____

    c. What effect does this have on those around you? _____

    _____

    d. Is this all that is required for evangelism, or is it a good place to start? _____

    e. Can you effectively share the Gospel if your life does not reflect the Gospel? _____

2. Look for/create opportunities to bring up the Gospel in everyday conversation.

    a. John 4:7 What did Jesus use here to bring up the Gospel?

    _____

    _____

    b. Matthew 24:1-2 What did Jesus use here to bring up the Gospel? _____

3. A few good lean-in questions:

    a. What is most meaningful in your life?

    b. How do you deal with problems in life?

    c. Do you believe in God?

    d. Do you go to church anywhere?

e. Would you go to Church with me?

f. Can we study the Bible together sometime?

g. Do you think God has a plan for your life?

h. Can you trust God with your future?

i. If you were to die tonight, are you sure you would go to Heaven?

Securing the Study

1. "When is the best time to get together?"

    a. Give them two choices.

    b. Make your schedule fit theirs!

2. "Where is the best place for you?"

    a. Your home or theirs.

    b. It is ideal to study in both places during the course of study. This will help to cement a closer bond of friendship.

3. Decide what method of study you will use.

4. Decide who will go with you.

    a. Will you lead the study or be the silent partner?

    b. If the prospect is of the opposite sex, do not go alone!!!!

5. IF you cannot secure a study, THEN offer a correspondence course, a Searching for Truth DVD & workbook, etc.

Guarantees:

1. Evangelism is difficult work.

2. Evangelism is highly rewarding.

3. The hardest part is getting started.

4. You will learn a great deal.

5. Teaching one person will create a desire to do more.

6. This will change your life and your perspective.

7. God will be pleased (Proverbs 11:30, Matthew 25:23).

8. God will help you do HIS work (Matthew 28:20).

Go!

New Christian Questionnaire

Information for the Church Directory

Name

_____

Physical Address

_____

_____

Mailing Address

_____

_____

Home Phone

_____

Cell Phone

_____

Email

_____

Birthday

_____

Anniversary

_____

Questions

1. What was your religious background before your conversion?

2. **What do you hope to gain from this study?**

Please list below any questions that you may have concerning any Biblical or religious subject: